The STRONG SENSITIVE BOY

Help Your Son Become a Happy, Confident Man

TED ZEFF, PH.D.

Foreword by Elaine Aron, Ph.D.

Prana Publishing

Publisher's Note

This publication is designed to provide accurate and authoritative information in regard to the subject matter covered. It is sold with the understanding that the publisher is not engaged in rendering psychological, financial, legal, or other professional services. If expert assistance or counseling is needed, the services of a competent professional should be sought.

Cover design by Jeremy Nieves
Edited by Carole Honeychurch
Text design by Jeremy Nieves

ISBN 0-9660745-2-9

Prana Publishing

First Printing

Author's Note

All of the stories in this book are based on my interviews of thirty highly sensitive men from five countries and from my clinical experience working with sensitive males. However, names, places and other details have been changed to protect the privacy of those individuals described in the book.

Contents

Foreward

It is my special joy to write this, and to commend you for having this book in your hands, because rarely is there a book that has as much potential to improve a boy's life as this one does. Research, including my own, makes it clear that sensitive children growing up in a stressful, nonsupportive environment are more likely to grow up to be depressed, anxious, shy, and unhealthy than nonsensitive children raised in a similarly poor environment. What is more significant, however, is the finding that sensitive children raised in an enriched, supportive environment are actually more resilient, happy, healthy, and socially competent than nonsensitive children raised in the same type of beneficial environment. These boys are an asset that is waiting to be developed.

In the sort of experiments we cannot do with humans, the same phenomenon has been found with rhesus monkeys. While those with this trait tended to grow up to be "uptight" when raised by average mothers, when given at birth to skilled mothers, these youngsters often grew up to be the leaders of their troop. If your sensitive boy grows up to be a leader of one of our "troops," that could be good for all of us.

The potential advantages with which your son was born are due to the basic characteristic of this innate trait: Sensitive individuals process experiences more thoroughly than others do. You probably already know this. Your son likes to observe before entering into things, notices subtleties, and reflects on possible outcomes when others may not. You may not have thought about the fact that his "style" allows him to gain much more from an enriched environment, and also from the cues, some of them subtle, that tell children that they are secure and loved. With this assurance, they can relax and learn. At school, with the right teacher, sensitive children can also learn even better than others, with a keener sense of what is expected of them. (Those who study the gifted see sensitivity and giftedness as almost the same thing.) For your son, the right environment is everything.

Stop Worrying—You're Doing Fine

Don't panic that maybe you have not been providing a good enough environment for your son. The simple fact that you are reading this book means that all along you have been striving to be attuned to him, which is the most important part of parenting. It shows him that you recognize who he is and want to help him. Whatever you have done in the past, with this book you will be fully prepared to help him gain the most from his sensitivity in the future. There is one catch here, however. You do not completely control his environment.

Raising a Boy in a Culture Hostile to Sensitivity

As Ted Zeff's interviews with sensitive men demonstrate, cultures differ widely in how they view sensitive men and boys. Many of you live in a society that disdains sensitivity, so that sensitive boys are bullied and hurt and misunderstood in a thousand ways, sometimes no matter how hard you try to prevent it. Grown men fear the very word "sensitive" might be applied to them. For example, in my research, sensitive men score lower on the Highly Sensitive Person Scale in spite of how much we tried to make it gender-neutral. Each item was tested to see if men answered True less often than women did. We only used the items that men and women answered equally often. Still, men's scores were lower. We have to presume that as men proceed down the list of items, they unconsciously check fewer, fearing they are being backed into the dangerous position of not seeming like a real man.

Both Ted and I have noticed that when someone from the media is interviewing us about this trait, if it is a man, he will almost always start to laugh nervously. He will usually vehemently deny being sensitive himself and ask skeptical questions meant to be humorous or scathing. To Ted and me, this is disturbing and sad. You can try it yourself. Bring up sensitivity in a group of men and chances are you will see all too well the reality of this cultural complex. You will also probably become clearer about the kind of culture you would like to live in and help create.

Let's Be Frank—Is Sensitivity in Males Really About Being Feminine?

Ted Zeff does a wonderful job of discussing all sides of the issue of whether sensitive men are more like women than other men are, but I can add a little from my own experience. In my research using North American samples only, where prejudice against sensitivity in men is strong, the effect of a poor parental environment was found to be greater for sensitive men than for other men, but it had similar effects on all women. One would think only sensitive women would be affected. This suggests to me that all women, along with sensitive men, are being harmed by their social environment, while nonsensitive males are being treated so well in it that they are hardly affected at all by a negative childhood.

There is another reason why sensitive men seem to be like women in certain ways. One of my interests is following the research on the discovery of "animal personalities." Sensitivity, or something given a similar name, has now been found in over 100 species. It is always a minority and always appears as an inherited strategy of observing more before acting. This caution is not fear, but might be thought of as exploring mentally to see what is out there before taking the risk of exploring physically. This is in contrast to the majority, who act faster, take more risks, are usually more aggressive, and learn less from their experience. They often get what they want, but at a cost, in that their impulsiveness can get them into trouble.

The minority, by being more cautious about the presence of predators and not being so aggressive about status, can avoid serious injury or death. They may be forced to look for food while the others eat what is easy to find, but in times of scarcity they know places to find nourishment that those with higher status have not learned about. (Interestingly, those with the trait of sensitivity will always be in the minority. In my example, if the majority of animals knew where food could be found during a famine it would no longer be an advantage. It's the same for us humans in a traffic jam. If only a minority of drivers knows of a short cut, it benefits that minority. If too many people know the same short cut, it isn't one anymore.) What about male behaviors specifically? In some species the males belonging to the minority wait for the majority, the tough guys, to wear themselves out fighting and then go off with females who have often preferred them anyway. Why might females favor less-aggressive males? All females, sensitive or not, have to adopt a cautious, self-protective strategy, because they will raise relatively few offspring carrying their DNA, and thus invest enormous energy in bearing, feeding, and raising them, while in many species one male may have hundreds of offspring over a lifetime. So we see that women, like sensitive men, have a general strategy of saving energy and being more cautious, aware of subtleties, and so forth. wA less-violent mate is less likely to injure the female or her offspring.

However, in many other crucial ways sensitive males are of course the same as other males: in how they are designed and in their hormones and behaviors. Hence I have sometimes said there are really four genders—nonsensitive males, sensitive males, nonsensitive females, and sensitive females (who are still more observant and cautious than other females). Or, better, I think the definition of what is masculine in humans should expand to include all types of men, as seems to be the case in cultures that admire gentleness, careful consideration before acting, nonaggression, and conscientiousness as much or more than they value the virtues of nonsensitive men.

Maybe right now you are thinking as I am: The world and all of its people and species would be better off if every culture valued gentle thoughtfulness in its men. If the creation of peace and justice is a type of cottage industry in which many of us take part, then your part will be raising a sensitive boy who can become a "leader of his troop." In the process you may cause others to see not only your son's true worth, but the worth of all who are highly sensitive. That will be a significant contribution towards reducing the power of those who are greedy, violent, and act on impulse without considering the long-term costs for the rest of us. So while you read this book, enjoy how much good may come of it.

–Elaine N. Aron, Ph.D.
Author of *The Highly Sensitive Person*
and *The Highly Sensitive Child*

Acknowledgments

I want to especially thank the thirty highly sensitive men that I interviewed for this book. The information that they shared about growing up as a sensitive boy was invaluable. I am so grateful to Elaine Aron for her enthusiastic support for my writing of this book and for her continued research, writing, and speaking on the trait of high sensitivity that she developed. I want to especially acknowledge my editor, Carole Honeychurch, for her brilliant editing skills and sagacious advice and Jeremy Nieves for his creative design of the book cover and the text. I am so thankful to my spiritual teacher, Amma, whose unconditional love for all humanity has inspired me and millions of others to live a more compassionate, balanced, and joyful life.

Introduction

According to Elaine Aron, acknowledged expert in the field and author of *The Highly Sensitive Person,* a highly sensitive person is one who is aware of subtleties in their surroundings and more easily overwhelmed when they have been exposed to a highly stimulating environment for too long (1996). Since approximately twenty percent of the population is highly sensitive and the trait is equally divided between males and females, many boys have a finely tuned nervous system.

The sensitive boy who reacts deeply to stimuli and exhibits emotional sensitivity is perfectly normal. However, there's something wrong with a society that shames males who do not act in a tough, aggressive, and emotionally repressed manner—especially when such a significant portion of the population simply isn't cut out for or comfortable with these behaviors. When sensitive boys do not conform to the stereotypical "boy code" and instead express compassion, gentleness, and vulnerability, they are frequently ostracized and humiliated. In this book, you will learn hundreds of methods for your son to survive and flourish in a culture that shames sensitive males. In addition, you will be empowered to help your son begin to appreciate his inborn trait of sensitivity and embrace the special benefits of being a sensitive male.

Though I frequently use the term "your son," this book is not only for parents of sensitive boys. It's just as important for other family members, such as grandparents, older siblings, and other relatives to understand and appreciate the sensitive boy. Anyone working with sensitive males (such as teachers, counselors, and mentors) need to be aware of how to help this large minority of boys.

And though much of the information is aimed at school-age boys, this book is also important for sensitive men to read. It will help them heal their childhood wounds, learn how to navigate through our aggressive, overstimulating world, and accept themselves as sensitive men. Finally, this book is also important for sensitive women. When I recently presented data from this book at a highly sensitive person (HSP) gathering in Colorado, I noticed that the women there were just as engaged in the discussion as the men. After all, how society treats sensitive men deeply affects highly sensitive women—and all women close to these extraordinary men and boys.

Why I Wrote this Book

When I was a little boy I always thought there was something wrong with me for not acting like other boys. As a sensitive boy, I reacted deeply to being teased in school and harshly disciplined at home, and this caused me a great deal of emotional pain, anxiety, and stress. I spent much of my childhood and adult life denying who I was in order to be accepted by the eighty percent "nonsensitive" American culture.

My family thought my sensitivity was strange, and my differences from others in my family prevented me from feeling like I fit in. As far back as I can remember I always abhorred violence. As a five year-old listening to Sergei Prokofiev's musical symphony for children, *Peter and the Wolf*, I became extremely upset when the wolf killed the duck in the musical story. I couldn't understand why no one else in my family was distraught, and I remember my mother laughing, telling me that it was only a make-believe story and that I shouldn't let it bother me. I lived on a very busy street for part of my childhood, and the noise from buses and trucks going by greatly disturbed me. I remember holding my hands over my ears, trying to escape from the constant ear-splitting, shrill noises. However, my parents were oblivious to the cacophony of grating sounds coming from the nearby road and couldn't understand why the noise would bother me.

Due to societal mores, males are not supposed to express emotions such as fear and sadness, and they're told that they shouldn't let anything bother them. Therefore, the trait of sensitivity is particularly challenging for boys. I've noticed a huge prejudice against the idea of the sensitive male, illustrated beautifully by the male talk-show host who interviewed me and uncomfortably made jokes about sensitive males and the major book publisher who told me that there is such a stigma against sensitive males that no one would want to buy a book with those words in the title. While there have been many books recently written about boys' emotional health, virtually none of the books have addressed the subject of sensitive boys. It's time for society to recognize that twenty percent of our boys have a finely tuned nervous system, and to give them the support, skills, and love that they need to grow into strong, happy, confident men.

What You Will Learn

In *The Strong, Sensitive Boy* I will offer hundreds of practical methods to help the sensitive boy navigate our nonsensitive world. In researching the subject of sensitive males, I performed in-depth interviews with thirty highly sensitive men from five countries. Although my study included a small sample, and a larger sample of sensitive males needs to be studied to obtain statistically significant data, the initial interviews indicated many interesting results, which have been useful in understanding what a sensitive boy needs.

I have discovered that many sensitive men have suffered emotionally from not fitting into the conventional boy culture, and consequently, many sensitive men experience low self-esteem. Based on my research, my work as a psychologist with sensitive males, and personal experiences, I've created many innovative and pragmatic coping strategies for parents, teachers, and families to use in helping the sensitive boy.

You will learn how western society teaches males to repress emotions and the biological causes for boys' behavior. I will offer many techniques to help your son work with and appreciate his sensitivity. And you may find it interesting to discover the different experiences of sensitive boys growing up in India, Thailand, Denmark, and North America.

We'll discuss the unique relationship between the sensitive boy and his mom and dad, as well as suggestions for how parents can support and nurture their sensitive boy. Then we will examine the challenges for the sensitive boy attending a public school and offer specific methods to help your son flourish in a large classroom. I'll address bullying at school and what parents and boys can do to stop it. Then you'll learn about some alternative educational settings that may be suited to your highly sensitive child.

We'll look at the unique challenges for sensitive boys in making and keeping friends, followed by suggestions on how your son can have satisfying friendships. Then you'll see how competitive team sports affect the sensitive boy and how to help your son participate in physical exercise that will increase his self-esteem. In addition, I will offer many suggestions to help increase your son's feelings of self-worth by improving his body image, boosting his health, and developing his innate spirituality.

We'll explore how your son can successfully and joyfully live with his deep emotions and discuss both therapeutic and nontherapeutic modalities to help the sensitive boy's emotional health. Then we'll look into some of the distinctive challenges of the teenage and young adult sensitive male, such as dating, going to college, and entering the world of work.

Near the end of the book, I've listed and answered questions from parents of sensitive boys and from teenage and young adult sensitive males. Some of the questions include: dealing with a boy who wants to always stay home, a teacher who ignores a boy's sensitivity, and a teenager's dating problems. The final chapter contains responses from thirty sensitive men from five different countries to the question: "What could your parents, teachers, and the other adults in your life have done differently that would have helped you to have had a more positive childhood?"

My wish is that this book will help thousands of sensitive boys grow into secure, happy, emotionally healthy men.

Chapter 1

Challenges and Benefits for the Sensitive Boy

"I think there's something wrong with my ten-year-old son. He cries easily, complains about loud noises in the house, and frequently covers his nose when I'm cooking in the kitchen. My son always stays home playing games on the computer, watching TV, or reading, and he has no friends."

"I always felt different as a boy since I didn't act like the other guys. When I saw boys fighting I would get nervous and feel afraid. I've always held back expressing my real feelings for fear of being shamed for being too sensitive."

If any of this sounds familiar, your son may be a highly sensitive boy. While your son may be different than most boys, he certainly is not alone. As previously mentioned, approximately twenty percent of the population is highly sensitive and the trait is equally divided between males and females (Aron, 1996). In other words, approximately twenty percent of all males are highly sensitive, or one out of every five boys has a finely tuned nervous system.

What Is a Highly Sensitive Boy?

What is the difference between a highly sensitive boy and a non-highly sensitive boy? A highly sensitive boy has trouble screening out stimuli and can be easily overwhelmed by noise, crowds and time pressure. The highly sensitive boy (HSB) tends to be very sensitive to pain and violent movies. He is also made extremely uncomfortable by bright lights, strong smells and changes in his life.

The highly sensitive boy's nervous system is "wired" in such a way that he is more acutely aware of, and attuned to, himself, other people, and his environment than the non-HSB. As a result, a highly sensitive boy is more easily stimulated by his surroundings. This is an inborn trait that researchers have also observed in approximately twenty percent of animal populations.

The highly sensitive boy generally reacts more deeply and exhibits more emotional sensitivity than the non-HSB. However, the degree of emotional and physiological reactions varies in each boy. For example, one HSB may not be bothered by noise or crowds, but is made uncomfortable by strong smells or wearing scratchy fabrics. Another boy may be extremely disturbed by loud noise and remain unbothered by watching violence on television. Although the trait has a high correlation with introversion, approximately thirty percent of HSBs are extroverts.

Most sensitive boys tend to pause to reflect before acting and would not be considered risk-takers. This tendency can easily be understood as demonstrating a healthy caution. However, in most societies boys are frequently encouraged to engage in risky behavior and are praised when they do so, while more cautious behavior is regarded with shame. The HSB will notice potential danger sooner than the non-HSB and is very aware of safety issues. Interestingly, this sense of caution seems to be regarded highly in the animal kingdom. For instance, the sensitive horse that intuits danger first and is able to warn the other horses of potential danger becomes the leader of his group. This respect for the sensitive animal as leader is probably the reason why virtually no animals died in the tsunami several years ago.

Sensitive boys are generally less aggressive than the "average" boy and are at the opposite end of the spectrum from the very unemotional, aggressive, risk-taking non-HSBs. The HSB is conscientious, sensitive to his environment, and socially aware of others around him.

Although many cultures tend to categorize sensitive boys as being unusual or not normal, the trait is basically neutral. Life can be both satisfying and challenging for the boy with a finely tuned nervous system. For example, his responsible and careful approach to completing his schoolwork can make him an excellent student. However, he may spend an inordinate amount of time agonizing over whether he completes his assignments properly. Some of the characteristics of a highly sensitive child include the following (Aron, 2002):

- Startles easily
- Complains about scratchy clothing or labels against his skin
- Notices the slightest unusual odor
- Seems very intuitive
- Is hard to get to sleep after an exciting day
- Doesn't do well with big changes
- Asks lots of questions
- Notices the distress of others
- Prefers quiet play
- Is a perfectionist
- Is very sensitive to pain
- Is bothered by noisy places
- Considers safety before climbing high
- Performs best when strangers aren't present

If your son exhibits many of the characteristics stated above, he is probably a sensitive boy. However, even if your son has only a few of the traits, but they are prominent in his life, he may also be considered a sensitive boy.

The Highly Sensitive Boy in Society

There are many more challenges for HSBs than HSGs (highly sensitive girls) due to societal values that males should be aggressive, thick-skinned, and emotionally self-controlled, which is the antithesis of a highly sensitive boy.

Most boys are taught from an early age to act tough and repress their emotions. According to author William Pollock, whenever boys do not conform to the "boy code" and instead show their gentleness and emotions, they are usually ostracized and humiliated (1998). In particular, sensitive boys learn to deny their real selves in order to be accepted and approved of by their peers. This denial can create fear, anxiety, and low self-esteem.

Author Paul Kivel has written that boys are put into an "act-like-a-man box," which means that they must be aggressive, tough, strong, in control and active. Whenever males step out of the box, they are humiliated (1992). In their book *Raising Cain*, authors Dan Kindlon and Michael Thompson state that if boys express emotions such as fear, anxiety, or sadness, they are commonly seen as feminine, and the adults and other children in their lives typically treat them as though these emotions are abnormal for a boy (1999). Conversely, girls who express emotions are fulfilling others' expectations, which actually helps them be more accepted by other girls (Aron, 2002).

Males Learn to Repress All Emotions Except Anger

Given our societal norms, it may come as a surprise that newborn boys are actually more emotionally reactive than girls. One study showed that baby boys cry more than baby girls when they are frustrated; yet by the age of five, most boys suppress all their feelings except anger. However, even though boys are taught to maintain emotional control, measuring their heart rate or skin conductance (sweaty palms) in emotionally arousing situations demonstrates that there is no difference between boys' and girls' responses (Kindlon and Thompson, 1999). Boys have the same human needs as girls. For example, a kindergarten teacher who welcomes her students each day with hugs has a calming effect on the most disruptive boys since all boys have a basic need to be loved, cared for, and respected.

When boys act aggressively or are silent, it is accepted as normal; yet when they express normal levels of fear, anxiety, and sadness (which are considered "feminine" emotions), others treat them as abnormal.

The effect on males of having to conform to wearing a tough-guy mask creates suffering on both a personal and societal level and is particularly devastating for the sensitive boy, who has to try harder than the average boy to repress his emotions.

Violent male behavior may stem from the perpetrator's fear that they aren't behaving aggressively enough and may be thought of as feminine. However, as I mentioned before, the behavior that is associated with girls (actions that demonstrate empathy, sensitivity, compassion, and so on) are also natural male traits—they are simply not recognized as such in many societies. Anthropologists have demonstrated that in certain cultures violent male behavior is nonexistent, such as in the Semoi of Malaysia. Likewise, the Hutterite Brethen, the largest and most successful Christian communal group in the United States, has enjoyed more than 350 years without a murder. We may infer then that violence isn't natural for males but is a learned behavior (Kindlon and Thompson, 1999).

What Is Masculinity?

Many males become uncomfortable in discussions of male sensitivity, since this trait has been interpreted as feminine. In the common duality that strictly separates what is masculine and what is feminine in our culture, being compared too closely with the feminine will likely threaten a man's constructed sense of manhood.

Many males who are destroying their lives to feel "manly" are not acting like real men; rather, they are performing a distortion of a cultural stereotype. By disowning their sensitive side, many males become half a person (Pittman, 1994). The aggressive, nonemotional male needs to learn to emulate the behavior of the compassionate, emotionally sensitive male to become a fully functioning human being—acknowledging and honoring each of their human qualities instead of segregating most and aggrandizing a few.

Dan, a married sociology professor at a small college in the Bay Area, said, "I grew up in the 1970s and 1980s, when Sylvester Stallone and Arnold Schwarzenegger were the big heroes. Real men were supposed to be strong, tough, and silent. At an early age I realized that I wasn't masculine enough, because I didn't like to fight or play competitive sports. Virtually all of the emotional pain that I had growing up was due to my having a finely tuned nervous system. However, even though other kids made fun of me, I always believed that deep down every person knows the importance of being sensitive to other people's feelings. I think in every culture there are people who appreciate sensitivity in males."

Unfortunately, although most non-highly sensitive men are kindhearted, the aggressive traits of non-highly sensitive men are exalted by the media of most western societies. The stereotypical macho media heroes have only reinforced false beliefs of what it means to be a man. By emulating the worst characteristics of non-highly sensitive men, the values of the military and political leaders in the twentieth century have led to more than 100 million people being killed in wars (Tolle, 1999). Also, some of the non-highly sensitive male executives of major corporations have severely damaged the planet with indiscriminate oil drilling, clear-cutting of forests, and polluting the environment. Although your son may have been told that he is too sensitive, the truth is that the proliferation of insensitive values has created a world on the brink of disaster. Our only hope for saving the planet is for all males to learn to be sensitive and kind toward all sentient beings.

In order for a society to function at an optimal level, there has to be a balance between the highly sensitive male (HSM) and non-HSM styles. While most non-HSMs will be found among the soldiers and chief executive officers of large corporations, and the HSMs will more often be counselors, artists, and healers, I think HSMs can function in almost any occupation so long as they do it their way, thoughtfully and without unnecessary aggression. The point is, societies that ulti-mately succeed and flourish are the ones that honor both the aggres-sive warriors and the sensitive advisers. The sensitive male has an important mission, which is to balance the aggressive behavior of some nonsensitive males who treat humans, animals, and Mother Nature in a callous fashion.

As our societal view of masculinity slowly begins to change, I'm hoping that more space will be created for both men and women to appreciate empathy, vulnerability, and sensitivity in men. In the last few years there have been numerous books about protecting boys' emotional health, new anti-bullying programs have been implemented in many schools, and new male political leaders have become a role model for boys how to exude strength with compassion, understand-ing, and compromise.

While sensitive males may not be warriors fighting on foreign battlefields, their battles take just as much courage. Fighting to uphold righteousness in society, long the purview of sensitive men and women everywhere, takes a strong backbone and much fortitude. Personal and global peace can only be achieved through the resurrection of such masculine heroes as Jesus, Buddha, the Dalai Lama, Mahatma Gandhi, and Martin Luther King, Jr. It takes a strong man to speak the truth about morality, virtue and justice as these great spiritual leaders have done.

Biological Causes for Boys' Behavior

Though some of what we consider traditionally masculine behavior is certainly based on cultural and societal norms and constructions, there is a biological foundation for much of boys' behavior. Michael Gurian, renowned author of many books about boys' emotions, has written that due to the dominance of the hormone testosterone in boys' bodies, aggression and physical risk-taking are programmed and hardwired into boys. The quality and quantity of aggressive behavior depends on a boy's age and how he has been taught to channel it (2007).

Gurian further states that male testosterone-driven behavior first developed millions of years ago, when males needed more testosterone to reproduce. As a result, men evolved to produce more of the necessary testosterone. Studies have shown that male infants and young boys are generally more aggressive than their female counterparts. However, if traumatic stress on the mother inhibits testosterone release to the male fetus in utero, the boy could be born with fewer aggressive tendencies. This may partly explain why HSBs are generally less aggressive than most boys. However, further research is needed to determine if there is a correlation between testosterone level and the sensitive male.

Sensitive Males, Sensitive Brains

Male and female behavior is certainly influenced by hormones, but it may also relate to actual structural differences in the brains of men and women. Laurie Allen, a brain researcher at UCLA, has pointed out some of the differences commonly seen between male and female brains. For instance, there is an increased focus in the male brain's right hemisphere on spatial relationships and activity. Also, most boys don't read as well as girls due to a smaller corpus callosum, which also accounts for males having a more difficult time expressing feelings. When verbal skills are tested, much less of the male brain is used than the female brain. Finally, brain function may explain why many men are so task-oriented. When examining brains of men, researchers could see how the brain "turned on" to do a task then "turned off" when the task was complete (Gurian, 2007).

In his 2007 book *The Minds of Boys*, Gurian has also pointed out that the difference between the male and female brain is genetically programmed based on our millions of years as hunters and gatherers. As a hunter, the male brain developed better spatial capacities and de-emphasized emotive, empathetic, and verbal skills, which were less needed for men in that milieu. As the primary childcare providers and food gatherers, women needed a better sense of hearing, touch, and taste than the men, and therefore evolved to have brains that allowed for these improved traits in females.

Gurian also wrote, "The sensitive boy has a 'bridge brain' and may show lower testosterone levels in the blood as well as higher oxytocin levels; thus his basic biology may be formed less toward the search for self through aggression and more for empathic bonding. He will also quite often show higher than average verbal development, more active word centers, and pathways in both hemispheres of the cerebral cortex. Furthermore, he may show more developed neural pathways for emotional signals in the brain. His corpus callosum may be larger than normal for a male, allowing more crosstalk between hemispheres of his brain and thus more emotional processing. In these ways his brain may be a 'bridge' between genders" (2007).

Simon Baron-Cohen, professor at Cambridge University in the fields of psychology and psychiatry and the author of *The Essential Difference: Male and Female Brains and the Truth About Autism*, showed that one in five males (approximately twenty percent) has what he calls a "female brain." This term is not used to suggest sexual preference, but to point out the broad continuum of gender in the brain (Baron-Cohen, 2004).

However, according to Elaine Aron, even if theoretically sensitive males have more of a female brain (that is, less testosterone and more oxytocin), then they should be similar to all females. However, only twenty percent of females are highly sensitive, not every female with a typically feminine brain. This discrepancy may indicate that what makes a male highly sensitive may be something other than the biological factors we've been examining. Highly sensitive males and highly sensitive females probably have more in common neurologically with each other than sensitive males have with the eighty percent non-highly sensitive female population. Dr. Aron also suggests that perhaps it is culture more than science leading researchers to determine that the sensitive male has a "female" brain. The duality of "male" and "female" as complete opposites is fundamental in our culture, so we are likely to conclude that anything not typically male must therefore be female, as if by default. In addition, while initial research indicates that one in five males have a brain structure that is different from most other males, further research is needed to determine if these males also have a finely tuned nervous system. In the end, we may find that what makes these men highly sensitive is neither something biologically typically "male" or typically "female," but something neurologically "sensitive."

Since most sensitive males not only react strongly to stimuli but also feel emotions deeply, the correlation between the sensitive male and non-highly sensitive females may be related more to these men's emotional reactions rather than biological similarities. However, we also have to take into consideration the cultural bias against males expressing emotions when considering similarities between sensitive male and female emotional reactivity. As we know, there is a strong stigma against men expressing emotions other than anger. In fact, Dr. Aron's research demonstrated that even highly sensitive men reported that they cried less frequently than highly sensitive women.

Even though the male brain may have been genetically programmed to foster the aggressive hunter, in ancient days some men must have expanded their consciousness beyond the daily hunt to help the human race evolve. The first person to begin writing hieroglyphics may have been a sensitive man who dropped out of the hunting party one day to utilize his innate traits of intuition, imagination, and creativity. Sensitive men may have also been at the forefront in the transition from a hunter-gatherer society to a more peaceful agrarian society.

Not Fitting In

Since the eighty percent of non-HSBs are hardwired neurologically to behave in a different manner than the twenty percent of HSBs, highly sensitive boys do not fit in with the vast majority of boys. Unfortunately, most HSBs have internalized the false belief that there is something wrong with them because they behave differently from most of their peers. As they grow and become socialized, they begin to see their innate gentleness, emotionality, and tendency toward overstimulation as abnormal and wrong.

This trend is reflected in my in-depth research with thirty highly sensitive men. Ninety percent of these men felt that their childhood was marked by feelings of alienation—that they didn't fit in with other boys. As I've mentioned, although my study included a small sample and a larger sample of sensitive men needs to be completed to obtain statistically significant data, the initial results indicate these feelings are common among HSMs. Even some of the highly sensitive males who reported that their parents supported their sensitivity and that they had positive peer interactions felt there was something wrong with them. Sadly, when sensitive children begin to think there is something wrong with them, they begin to shut down and suppress all of the positive traits related to their sensitivity (Crawford, 2009).

Most boys like to play in a rough and tumble manner and seem to enjoy watching combative scenes in movies and television. However, my research indicated that eighty-five percent of sensitive men always avoided fighting as a boy and ninety percent did not like watching violence on television or in the movies. Frequently, boys who don't want to fight are humiliated by their peers, which contributes to poor self-esteem. Dan, the highly sensitive man we met earlier, told me that when he used to go to the movies with his friends as a boy, he would pretend to really enjoy the bloody and violent scenes while secretly looking away from the screen. He was always afraid that the other boys would see him avoiding the screen and tease him, encouraging him to feel that there was something wrong with him

Aaron was brought up in a rural area in Eastern Canada with five brothers and sisters, an overwhelmed mother, and a strict father. He told me, "I felt like something was wrong with me since I didn't fit in with my family. I was a perfect example of a highly sensitive person as described in the books I've read on the subject. As a boy, I was very sensitive to cold, couldn't have tags on the back of my shirts, and had to have clothes that fit just perfectly. My parents didn't understand me and considered me 'spoiled.' For example, I could tell when bread had a slightly moldy taste and wouldn't eat it, yet everyone else in the family thought there was nothing wrong with it. They thought I was crazy. Even when, the next day, you could physically see the mold, they were still not convinced that I could taste the mold the day before."

Some HSMs who were regularly humiliated by peers, teachers, and family while growing up have developed post-traumatic stress disorder. Terry, who was raised in a middle-class Long Island suburb twenty miles from New York City, had parents who not only didn't support his sensitivity, but would tease him for it. Terry reported, "My father was a typical macho man who would humiliate me for my sensitivity, calling me a 'baby girl' whenever I cried or got upset. I became a frightened boy, avoiding other children at school out of fear of being hurt, and I used to hide in my room to avoid being abused by my dad. As a child I felt as if I were walking around with no skin—sort of like a sponge, absorbing everything that came my way. I had no protection from the endless attacks directed at me at home, school, or in my neighborhood. This embattled existence eventually shattered my self-esteem and created PTSD."

Being humiliated for having a finely tuned nervous system is like experiencing discrimination based on the color of your skin, your religion, or your national origin. As with other minority groups, it's important for sensitive males and their parents, family, and friends to educate the general population about themselves. Although the sensitive boy may be different from most other boys, it's crucial that adults recognize and support the HSB's unique traits, helping him navigate through a majority non-HSP world that tends to value aggressive, risk-taking behavior amongst boys.

Positive Traits of the Sensitive Male

The highly sensitive boy may have trouble fitting into the narrow mold of a stereotypical male, but he has many wonderful qualities. Some of these include:

- Compassion
- Gentleness
- The ability to act as a peacemaker
- Concern about the humane treatment of animals

- A sense of responsibility
- Conscientiousness
- Creativity
- The tendency to feel love deeply
- A great intuitive ability
- An awareness of his unity with all beings
- The ability to have and appreciate deep spiritual experiences

Although your HSB may not fit in with many boys in our competitive, overstimulating, and often violent world, the sensitive boy tends to share many of the characteristics of the great male spiritual teachers. These men also had trouble fitting in with aggressive, combative males and were sometimes humiliated for their empathetic and compassionate behavior. And of course, this inability to fit in gave them the opportunity to do great things.

Although you may not think of your son as a future saint, it would be beneficial to spend some time reflecting on the qualities I listed above. Your HSB shares these with the truly great spiritual giants who have walked the Earth.

All of the HSMs in my study indicated that throughout their life they "usually" or "always" have been: intuitive, gentle, responsible, a peacemaker, and good at counseling people. Your son is in good company, sharing these traits with such famous highly sensitive males as Abraham Lincoln; the great psychologist Carl Jung; and Wolfgang Amadeus Mozart.

Recognizing these positive tendencies and abilities in your boy will give you the opportunity to support and even celebrate them. Many parents really appreciate and support their sensitive sons, joining in to share their interest in reading, art, and quiet games. Children of such supportive parents develop high self-esteem. These parents are thrilled that their highly sensitive sons will help to uphold the highest values in society.

Sensitive Males Enjoying Their Sensitivity

Virtually all of the HSMs in my study enthusiastically shared with me how much they appreciated the positive aspects of being sensitive. For example, many men discussed how their intuition and ability to notice subtleties in the environment has helped strengthen their relationships.

Hans, a married teacher from Denmark with two young children, told me that being sensitive to subtle energy has really helped him thrive. "Being a highly sensitive man has made me a good listener, and I can understand other people's needs. The empathy that I feel helps me to open my heart so I can easily feel love for people. I have a deep inner sense about what is the right thing to do in most situations. It's kind of like all the answers I seek are contained in my inner body."

Jonathan, a married financial adviser from Philadelphia with a teenage daughter, felt similarly: "I enjoy the advantage of having an abundance of common sense due to my deep thinking capabilities. I also have a strong sense of right and wrong, and I'm highly intuitive, which allows me to know what people want and need. I feel that my sensitivity has helped me become successful in my profession of financial advising."

Alan, a married psychologist from Pittsburgh with three young children, told me, "Many people want to see me for counseling since I understand and recognize how people around me feel and sense what they need. People trust my judgment and feel safe knowing that they won't be criticized. My ability to express my feelings has given me great joy, helping me to experience life more fully. Because I'm able to deeply feel and express my emotions, I feel that I've helped make society a gentler, more loving place. Also, my sensitivity creates a more enriching marriage because I'm sensitive to my wife's needs and I'm always trying to improve the relationship. I feel that sensitive males are considered a good catch, whether as a friend, in business or in a romantic relationship."

Doug, a divorced electrician from Los Angeles, told me how his sensitivity has helped him with mechanical issues. "I believe that my sensitivity includes having a better tactile sense than other men, which gives me an advantage when a delicate touch is needed. For example, it has helped when landing a plane, driving, and performing other tasks that require refined movement and dexterity. I'm extremely aware of slight abnormalities, so I am able to fix things before they become a major problem. This awareness includes everything from hearing poor bearings on my vehicles to smelling small gas leaks."

Sensitive men also experience deep joy from their involvement in the arts and creative endeavors. Jeffrey, a social worker from Chicago, said, "I really look forward to coming home from the office and working on my pottery wheel. While working in my studio, I usually listen to classical music. When I'm listening to Mozart and creating my ceramics, I can easily feel deep joy as my problems disappear."

Peter from San Diego is a married musician and the father of a two-year-old boy. Peter also experiences deep joy from his artistic endeavors: "I deeply enjoy making music, listening to the sounds and the subtleties of rhythm and texture. What a gift my sensitivity is!"

When sensitive males feel free to experience their sensitivity, they discover the joys of their finely tuned senses. And when they are allowed to flourish, helped by family and friends, they know the peace of self-acceptance.

Sensitive Boys Are Not All the Same

There is a wide continuum of behavior within the eighty percent non-HSBs, and there is a variety of emotional and physiological reactions that each sensitive boy exhibits. While most sensitive boys abhor violence, one HSM told me that when he was a boy he loved hunting with a BB gun.

Dr. Elaine Aron describes how some people (both highly sensitive and non-highly sensitive) are high-sensation seekers who enjoy stimulating activities and are easily bored (1996). These high-sensation seekers often like physical thrills and love to explore. It's possible for your son to be an HSB and a high-sensation seeker as well. Later in the book you will meet an HSM who enjoyed playing ice hockey as a boy and exploring new terrain. Parents need to be aware that the HSB high-sensation seeker can still be easily overwhelmed by stimuli and may need an extra amount of downtime after participating in his adventurous activities.

The Myth that Sensitive Males Are Gay

In most societies, being sensitive is generally associated with feminine behavior, which can be quite emasculating for the sensitive male. Gary, a middle-aged married physician from Atlanta, told me, "For much of my life I did things to appear more manly in order to avoid the stigma of being too effeminate. Lately I have become more open and less guarded with close friends, but I still remain somewhat cautious with most men. I think the biggest way our society shames sensitive males is by calling their masculinity into question. The more sensitive you behave, the more likely someone is going to assume you are gay."

Tom, a married small-business owner with an adult son from Providence, Rhode Island stated, "My sexuality has always been straight. But, throughout my life, many people thought I was gay since I was gentle and never enjoyed the typical rough interactions among guys. On numerous occasions I've been shamed by my dad and by boys in school for not acting 'manly,' whatever that's supposed to mean."

Most HSMs in my study reported that they were concerned that they weren't masculine enough and were worried that others may have thought that they were effeminate or gay. But there are at least two big problems with the implied correlation of sensitivity, femininity, and homosexuality. First, my research and experience shows that most HSMs identify as heterosexual. Ninety-five percent of the HSMs in my survey are straight. This initial data may indicate that there is no correlation between having a finely tuned nervous system and sexual identity.

Second, correlating sensitivity with the feminine and further correlating femininity with homosexuality is extremely problematic. As long as we subscribe to this notion of duality—in which "sensitive" equals "feminine" and "gay" equals "feminine" (and feminine is seen as negative), we are restricting ourselves from seeing the full range of humanity, trapping ourselves in a structure that isolates us and humiliates those who do not conform to our overly restrictive norms. These notions of gender and sexual identity create problems for most of us (who, after all, fits perfectly into any of these narrow boxes?), and particularly for the highly sensitive man and boy. HSMs and HSBs are male—truly male—and it is the dualistic and negating ideas about what is feminine and what is masculine that need to broaden to allow for variation.

There is also a misperception that most gay males are highly sensitive. This is another stereotype that tends to restrict our view of humanity. There is no current data to support the belief that gay men have a finely tuned nervous system. Even those homosexual men who are seen to behave in very "feminine" ways are not necessarily highly sensitive. This is just a manifestation of the correlation of sensitivity with the feminine. Anecdotal information suggests that most homosexual males are probably not negatively affected by noise, bright lights, and crowds any more than heterosexual males.

However, gay males with a finely tuned nervous system have a particularly challenging time since they don't fit in with the eighty percent non-highly sensitive males and they are also different from the vast majority of the heterosexual male population. Gay highly sensitive boys need special love and support by parents, extended family members, teachers, and the entire community to counteract the negative societal stigma toward homosexuality and sensitive men in general. The way in which parents or guardians respond to a youth's sexual orientation profoundly influences the child's mental health, according to researchers at San Francisco State University whose findings appeared in the January 2009 *Journal of the American Academy of Pediatrics*. Young gay people whose parents or guardians responded negatively when they revealed their sexual orientation were more likely to attempt suicide, experience severe depression, and use drugs than those whose families accepted the news (Ryan, et al).

Writer Dustin Lance Black, who wrote the screenplay of the movie *Milk*, offered an impassioned tribute to young gay people at the 2009 Academy Awards:

"If Harvey Milk had not been taken from us thirty years ago, I think he would want me to say to all the gay and lesbian kids out there tonight who have been told they are less than by the churches, by the government, by their families, that you are beautiful, wonderful creatures of value, and that no matter what anyone tells you, God does love you and that very soon, I promise you, you will have equal rights across this great nation of ours."

All of us, in our myriad differences, need to feel this kind of acceptance and self-worth. So, rather than encouraging your highly sensitive son to try to squeeze himself into an ill-fitting box, encourage him to embrace and make good use of the differences that make him unique.

Sensitive Males Around the World

While biological factors may influence the behavior of boys, what a particular society values is an equally important factor in determining how the sensitive boy is treated. For example, a study of Canadian and Chinese school children concluded that highly sensitive children in Canada were the least liked and respected, while Chinese sensitive children were the most popular (Chen, et al., 1992).

In countries like Thailand, where the positive attributes of sensitive males are recognized, the HSB is often given a leadership position, since others recognize his innate ability to help achieve the group's goals. Nui, a married lab technician who was raised in Thailand, told me that he was elected president of his class several times in grade school and high school. The sensitive male in many cultures has been recognized as an "intuitive priestly advisor" and has historically been granted special status for helping the community thrive (Aron, 1996).

Ashok, an engineering student from India, told me, "While I was growing up in India no one ever shamed me for being sensitive. In India, the men don't try to act as strong and tough as in the U.S. We see different role models in the media than in the U.S. For example, since I was a boy, I was a great fan of a movie actor in India named Amir Khan. He appeared sensitive and passionate in all his movies, opening his heart and forthrightly expressing his feelings. I don't think Amir Khan would be as popular in the United States since most of the American male movie stars always act so tough and never show their vulnerability."

Hans from Denmark mentioned, "Countries in Scandinavia are quieter than the United States. Loud and pushy behavior is generally looked down upon in Denmark. It's a consensus culture, and the Danes usually don't like very aggressive behavior. Even though I was sensitive as a boy, I felt that my parents, teachers, and peers treated me with respect."

When I took a recent trip to Denmark, I noticed how quiet it was in the large urban metropolis of Copenhagen. I was surprised to see so many men caring for children, working as preschool teachers and pushing baby carriages.

My study indicates that sensitive boys have a less challenging time growing up in certain Asian and European countries than in North America. However, anecdotal information suggests that growing up as a sensitive male could be as difficult in many other countries as in the United States. The HSMs from India, Thailand, and most HSMs from Denmark stated that they were never or rarely teased at school for their sensitivity. While some Danish HSMs said they experienced some disapproval for being a sensitive boy, the displeasure appeared to be less prevalent than that experienced by men growing up in North America. Subjects in the study also reported that teasing in those countries was usually done in a playful manner, which differed greatly from some of the malicious and cruel taunting that HSBs experienced in North America. Many North American sensitive men told me that they still have emotional scars from the physical and emotional humiliation that they experienced from their peers in school.

The Sensitive Boy in North America

North America is one of the most challenging places for the sensitive male to grow up and live in. Why should this be? Well, one theory is that the European men who originally ventured across the sea to explore and settle the new world were risk-taking, aggressive non-HSP males who fought the wilderness and the Native Americans. Sensitive men tended to remain behind in Europe, possibly serving as priestly advisers to royalty, creating artistic masterpieces, or writing divine musical sonatas. Perhaps this is why some countries in Northern Europe, like Denmark and Holland, are more accepting of the sensitive male compared to the United States. In many cultures, it is considered advantageous to be sensitive. For example, in cultures where people live close to the earth, the highly sensitive male herbalists and shamans are glorified.

Every North American HSM that I interviewed expressed dismay at how his country shames sensitive males. Gary aptly stated, "In America, I never felt like my culture honored or accepted sensitive men. I suppose the only form of appreciation for sensitive men in America comes in the creative spheres, such as music. It seems more acceptable for a man to be involved in music and be openly sensitive. However, even some famous musicians who appear too sensitive are ridiculed."

On the other hand, there is now a subculture of progressive people in America who accept and even cherish sensitivity in males. This changing attitude stands in sharp contrast to years past, when insensitivity was almost universally accepted as the norm for men. Unfortunately, American society is still saturated with violent video games and the ubiquitous brutal ultimate fighting and wrestling matches that have probably contributed to an increase in male violent behavior.

Conclusion

In this initial chapter, we've examined what the term "highly sensitive" actually means and some reasons why it exists in some boys and not in others. We've discussed the drawbacks to being a highly sensitive male in our western society and have also noted some of the wonderful attributes and possibilities for the HSB. We've also seen how differently HSMs are viewed in some other parts of the world, which reminds us of the socially constructed nature of what we think of as a normal, successful male. If what is valued in one country is not in another, it becomes clear that these values depend on your point of view. This is great news: it means that we can help change our society's viewpoint and thus our boys' experience within society.

In the following chapter, we'll look at the highly sensitive boy's relationship with a key figure in his life: his mom.

Chapter 2

The Sensitive Boy and His Mother

"Even though I had a rough time growing up as a sensitive boy, I knew that I could always count on my mom. Her unwavering support and love got me through all the difficult times."

"I remember that my mother would laugh at me for being afraid of going to the dentist. What I needed was her support when I was scared. If she had only known how much her put-downs hurt me, she probably wouldn't have made fun of my fears."

In this chapter we will discuss the challenges and joys of a mother raising a sensitive boy and point out the deleterious effects that an unsupportive mom can have on her son. We'll end with some suggestions for disciplining the sensitive boy and I'll present the most effective methods for a mom to support and nurture her sensitive son.

Secure Attachment

A positive and secure bond of attachment between mother and son is important in any family, but it is essential for the sensitive boy. When a mother reacts reliably and sensitively to her infant's needs, he will form a strong, positive bond with her (what is commonly called a *secure attachment*). This sense of stability fosters a resilient foundation of trust and love on which he can build other relationships (Kindlon and Thompson, 1999). In other words, experiencing this bond of trust and love early on with the mother allows a child to trust and love others more securely. However, many of us, highly sensitive and not, didn't experience this strong bonding early on. About forty percent of both children and adults have an insecure attachment style resulting from a lack of consistent and responsive maternal nurturance (Bowlby, 1973).

While insecure attachment is not more common among highly sensitive people, insecurity affects HSPs more adversely than non-HSPs (Aron, 2002). The sensitive male with an insecure attachment frequently meets new events with fear and feelings of being overwhelmed. Since sensitive boys particularly need to feel safe and protected, a secure attachment in infancy is an essential component to help a sensitive boy grow into a secure and confident man. I recommend reading *The Highly Sensitive Child*, in which Dr. Aron offers excellent suggestions for moms seeking to create a secure attachment for their sensitive children.

However, even if you fear that your attachment to your highly sensitive son may have been lacking in his infancy, there are many ways that you can support and bond with your son now. Later in this chapter, we'll be reviewing powerful techniques that will allow you to strengthen your bond with your son and help him thrive today.

Premature Separation from Mom

There is a societal myth that boys don't need as much love and protection as girls. Even with infant and toddler boys, there is a strong belief out there that we should encourage them to be tough and should avoid "coddling" them. Hence, boys are frequently forced to separate from their mothers too early as society encourages them to become physically and emotionally independent of mom at an early age. This pulling away can create many interpersonal problems for the boy later on, especially in intimate relationships with women. Without the model of a strong connection with the first important woman in their lives, some men who experienced a lack of early childhood nurturance don't quite know how to bond with women later on. Also, boys who are pushed to separate from their mothers too early may become depressed and anxious (Pollack, 1998). You may be all too familiar with the mother who emotionally pushes her son away too soon, hoping to avoid turning him into a "mama's boy."

According to author Michael Gurian, by the time most boys enter kindergarten they will have a pull toward separation and independence (1996). However, this may not be true for the sensitive boy, who may feel overwhelmed when he enters a large, noisy classroom. He may likely exhibit fear of leaving his mother when first entering school. It's important for moms to recognize how challenging it may be for their son to make the transition from being home with mom to entering a new preschool or kindergarten class. It's crucial that a mother lets her son take extra time to slowly integrate into the new environment if he feels overwhelmed and scared, rather than forcing him to be a "big boy" and expecting him to immediately join in with the other children.

However, if your son, for example, needs to attend pre-school due to your work schedule, potential difficulties can be ameliorated by a caring teacher and a sensitive mom. During the transition period you can stay with him at school and slowly increase the time that you are not in direct contact with him. You should also choose a small, less stimulating preschool where the teachers are understanding of your son's sensitivity and where he can develop a secure bond with the teachers.

Being a Supportive Mom

A highly sensitive boy will usually need more support and love from his mother than a non-HSB. Mom has a pivotal role in helping her son feel that he is a worthwhile human being, in spite of messages that he may receive from his peers, teachers, and the media that there is something wrong with him. At times this may feel like an added responsibility, but it's also a wonderful opportunity for moms to share a special closeness with their sons and actively participate in helping them flourish. Alan, the psychologist from Pittsburgh, told me, "I never had any problems with my sensitivity since, from an early age, I accepted myself as I was, even though I knew I was different. I think that I was able to love and accept myself because I had the support of a mother who unconditionally loved me and was always there for me."

Your sensitive son will easily notice subtleties in your interactions with him, so even if you are supportive of your son, it's important that he really knows that you deeply understand and appreciate his sensitivity. Joel, a married technology consultant from Terre Haute, Indiana remembered, "Even though I had a great mom, she didn't really understand me. She tried her best with me, but she just didn't get why I needed to spend so much time alone. She never said anything derogatory, but I intuitively felt that she thought I was strange since I wasn't like my brother or sister."

Dealing with Dad's Disapproval

Even when an HSB has the loving support and understanding of his mother, he may still be contending with a disapproving father. Some of the highly sensitive men I've worked with feel regret that their mothers wouldn't or couldn't deal more effectively with their son's father's reactions. The mom of an HSB can help mediate the relationship between her son and his dad. Although she may be unable to control the father's responses, a mom can try to manage the fallout of her son's damaged feelings.

Jeffrey shared his mother's love for the arts, and he recalled, "I used to go to classical music concerts with my mom, and she encouraged me to pursue art and other cultural activities. I remember that Mom gave me her watercolor art supplies, which I thoroughly enjoyed, while my father totally ignored my interest in art. While I basked in my mom's love and support and pursued the creative arts, my dad was disgusted with my artistic endeavors with my mom and would sometimes tease me for spending so much time with her instead of playing sports with the neighborhood boys like my brothers did. Even though she was supportive, she didn't protect me from my dad's condemnation of my artistic pursuits, which made me feel like I wasn't a real boy."

While Mom may not be able to change Dad's negative behavior toward their sensitive son, she can always carefully listen to how her son feels and help him understand why Dad may have difficulty accepting sensitivity in males. Throughout the book many suggestions will be given to show Mom how her sensitive son can cope with societal prejudice against sensitive boys.

Mom-and-Son Balance

One of the ways that a mother may try to mitigate the disapproval of the father is to try to fill the void herself. If Dad is not providing the love and support that she sees as necessary to her son's development, a mom may jump in and attempt to become her son's "good" parent. Instead of shielding her son from the father's scorn (which she may feel unable to do), she determines to erase the disapproval through bonding more deeply.

While this is an understandable reaction to a very difficult situation, this kind of unbalanced relationship between the mother and her son may not actually turn out to be in her son's best interests. It is psychologically important for boys to relate to and model themselves after a male role model so that they know how to behave as a man in our society. When sensitive boys have only a mother to relate to, they may begin to question their own essential masculinity, creating doubt and unease in their minds. (Finding your son a supportive male role model can go a long way toward ameliorating this problem, and I will discuss how and why to find one in more detail later in the book.)

Furthermore, some moms may find themselves using their relationship with their sons as a replacement of sorts for a healthy adult bond. A mom who doesn't have access to or hasn't cultivated close relationships with other adults, particularly with adult men, can sometimes substitute an overly close relationship with her son, making him "the man of the house." Single moms may be particularly vulnerable to creating this dynamic. And, unfortunately, these loose parental boundaries do a disservice to both the mother and her son. The mother is not prompted to go out and find a satisfying adult relationship, and the son feels an overwhelming responsibility to take care of his mother and misses out on the model of a healthy adult relationship.

Mothers of sensitive boys need to create a balance between giving her son the love and support he needs while encouraging him to pursue his own interests outside the home. Tom said, "Since my mom was also very sensitive, she understood and appreciated my sensitivity. However, I think that she became overly protective of me, which didn't help me learn how to cope with the aggressive world that I had to deal with every day at school. In retrospect, it probably would have been better for me to have been more involved in activities outside the home rather than spending so much of my childhood at home with Mom."

The situation that Tom found himself in is not all that uncommon for sensitive boys. Since many sensitive boys prefer to spend time at home, they may not learn how to relate with the eighty percent of nonsensitive children. A mom should encourage her son to engage in outside activities with other children while making sure that he feels safe in those ventures. Throughout the book we will discuss ways that Mom can make sure her son is safe outside the home.

As a sensitive eight year-old boy growing up in Atlanta Georgia, I remember wanting to play indoors rather than venturing outside where I was afraid that I would be hurt by neighborhood bullies. My mother didn't have a clue about why I wanted to stay home instead of going out to play. Luckily, when I was nine years old, we moved into a new house where I fondly remember playing outside with five other friendly boys on my street. A mother needs to pick up on the subtle cues why her son wants to stay indoors and know when to encourage him to interact more with other children. Since most boys would feel ashamed to tell their mom that they are afraid to go outside because of bullies, you may want to gently inquire if your son feels unsafe outside the home rather than just encouraging him to go outside. If he's not able to verbalize his feelings, listen carefully to subtle cues about why he doesn't want to go outside. Do remember that some HSBs and non-HSBs are homebodies who prefer to stay indoors.

A mom can't always protect her son from being hurt emotionally or physically, but she can let him know that she will always be there for him. When a mom encourages her sensitive boy, even if he has challenges outside the home, his mother's love and support will live in his heart forever, and he will be able to grow into a more confident man.

When Mom Disapproves

As I've mentioned, it's crucial for a sensitive boy to experience the unconditional love and acceptance of his mother. This strong foundation helps him to grow into an emotionally healthy man. Unfortunately, research shows that shy sons, including most sensitive boys, are often their mother's least favorite child (Aron, 2002). This may be because some mothers see their sons' shyness as the mom's failure, having internalized society's false belief that boys should be assertive, and these moms want to distance themselves from the effects of this (skewed) perspective. Regardless of the reason, the effects of a mother's disapproval can negatively impact the shy, sensitive boy's mental health. In my study, I noticed that the men who had supportive moms growing up had higher self-esteem and fewer emotional problems than the men whose moms were unsupportive.

Aaron, the married HSM from Canada with three children, remembered: "My mother was critical of my shy demeanor as a boy. She constantly criticized me for being too timid and would push me to spend more time with the aggressive boys in the neighborhood. She let me know that I shouldn't hang out with my only friend because he was also sensitive. She would pick on me, telling me that I was like a bump on a log when I stayed home. I remember her once yelling at me that I was such a sissy and ordering me to get out of the house and play with those 'normal boys' across the street. How do you think that made me feel? I still feel that pain deeply today as if it happened yesterday, even though it was forty years ago."

Accepting your son's sensitive trait should not be equated with feeling sorry for him for being sensitive. Doug from Los Angeles reported that while his mom acknowledged him for being a clever and compassionate boy, she told him that she also felt sorry for him for being so different from other boys. When a mom conveys, even subtly, that her son's trait is something abnormal, she is giving him the message that there's something wrong with him. Messages like these can significantly lower his self-esteem.

It's challenging enough for a non-HSB to grow up with an abusive mother, but for a sensitive boy, it can be devastating. Terry, a single bookkeeper from New York, told me how his mother's emotional and physical abuse resulted in him having difficulty sustaining a loving relationship with a woman throughout his life. "I grew up in a classic dysfunctional family where I had an absentee father who was always carousing around and a bitter, raging mother. She would take her anger at my dad out on my brother and me. However, my older brother would just laugh in her face when she started in on us. He would humiliate her right back even when she started slapping us.

"I, on the other hand, became mortally frightened of her rage and spent most of my childhood with my stomach tied up in knots, not knowing when the next outburst would occur. She basically scared the crap out of me. It felt like every cell of my body was full of her venom. I still notice that my muscles tighten and fists clench whenever I see an angry woman to this day. I have been very cautious about getting involved in relationships with women, and subsequently I've never really had a satisfying relationship. Most women don't understand why I need my space and have criticized me for not wanting to be with them as much as they want to spend time with me. Naturally, their complaints only drive me further away."

It doesn't take a psychologist with a Ph.D. to understand that if you put a sensitive little boy in the center of a room and constantly criticize and scream at him, he will probably shrink toward the corner of the room in fear. The timid little boy with a sensitive nervous system may never fully recover from a barrage of insults as he withers away in terror. However, if you were to tell that same little boy in a gentle, loving manner how good he is, appreciating everything about him, that little, sensitive boy would flourish, exuding self-confidence and joy.

Getting the Support of Other Women

It's challenging for even the best of mothers to be constantly supportive and accepting of her son's sensitivity. It takes the patience of a saint to be able to always exude unconditional love for your children. That's why they invented grandmas! Dan, the Bay Area sociology professor remembered, "My grandma lived next door to me while I was growing up, and she was always there for me when I felt lonely. When my mom was having a bad day and was on my case, I knew that I could always go to my grandma's house for some nurturance. Just thinking about her love for me makes me choke up with tears. Wow! I really miss her. I think that my grandma's love is the main reason I've been so successful and happy as a man." As Dan's story so eloquently illustrates, it's vital for your son to have other loving female support while he's growing up.

Michael Gurian emphasizes the need for a boy to belong to a tribe of three families. "The first family is the birth or adoptive parents, including grandparents; the second family is made up of extended families—blood relatives or non-blood friends, day-care providers, teachers, peers, and mentors; and the third family is the culture, community, media, church groups, government, other institutions, and influential community figures. In many cultures some kind of non-blood kin system is built into community life. However, since the 1950s, especially in North America, the nuclear family with no outside support has emerged as the dominant force where children are raised" (1996, 58).

This isolated form of childrearing, where the burden is placed on one or two frequently stressed-out adults can be disastrous, especially for the sensitive boy. The HSMs in my study who had positive, loving relationships with other adult females besides their mom reported having more positive experiences as a boy than those interviewees who did not have these additional relationships.

It's no surprise that the phrase "It takes a village to raise a child" has become so popular. An isolated nuclear family generally is unable to give any boy, let alone a sensitive boy, the full support that he needs. Parents should investigate and pursue opportunities for their son to receive maternal nurturance from other adult female figures besides Mom, including relatives, family friends, teachers, counselors, babysitters, and community figures. Not only will these relationships help your son, but they will help take the pressure off of Mom having to be unconditionally supportive all the time.

I think that perhaps one of the reasons that sensitive boys from India and Thailand reported experiencing happier childhoods than those from North America is due to the role of the extended family and community in raising children in those cultures. Michael Gurian recalls being raised for some years in India by extended-family members who treated him like their own child. He further reported that in India, it is considered crazy for a nuclear family to raise a child alone (1996). Tun, a medical student from Thailand, fondly remembered, "My grandmother and Aunt Pui, who both lived with us, always praised me when I was growing up. I believe that added support has made me feel more self-confident."

Quarreling Parents Hurt the Sensitive Boy

Many HSMs in my study recalled how horrific it had been for them listening to their parents arguing. Brian, a married accountant from Denver, initially stated that he had a pretty good childhood and described his parents as basically caring parents. However, later in our interview he remembered how scared he had been listening to his parents loudly quarreling with each other when he lay in bed at night. "I remember one incident when I was about five or six. I was lying in bed, feeling so frightened as my parents downstairs screamed and threatened each other. I heard something break and then the door slam.

I still remember holding on to my teddy bear and crying. I couldn't fall back to sleep, fearing that my mom or dad had left. I had nowhere to turn since it wouldn't have helped to go to my little sister's room, and I recall that I felt utterly helpless and scared."

Though any child may be alarmed and frightened by an experience like Brian's, highly sensitive children are likely to be affected even more by parental conflict. The sensitivity that is the hallmark of this trait means that these boys feel emotions very deeply and take their feelings to heart. So, while it's important to limit parental arguing in front of any child, it's even more crucial to protect the HSB from this kind of conflict.

Some HSMs in my study thought it was their responsibility to help their parents get along better. The responsible and intuitive HSB may inadvertently take on the role of marriage counselor for his parents. Steve, a married real estate appraiser from Boston, said, "I took my parents fighting very personally. I think I believed that I could fix their marriage and make them happy when they were miserable with each other. Parents should be helping their children, yet in my case, I ended up trying to fix my parents' marriage."

Parents need to be aware how their arguing can deeply disturb their sensitive child and take steps to make sure that their disagreements are not aired so loudly that their sensitive child hears them. Parents also need to keep their adult disputes private so that their sensitive child doesn't feel responsible for helping them get along.

Gentle, Firm Discipline by Mom

Some moms may have internalized the false societal belief that boys need stronger discipline than girls. However, your sensitive son can learn a lesson better when he is calm and receptive, so when you are disciplining your son it's vital to talk to him in a gentle manner. If mom screams at her sensitive boy when he misbehaves, he will become more frightened and upset by her anger than her non-HSC (highly sensitive child).

Sensitive boys generally tend to feel guilty when they make mistakes, so there is no need for harsh discipline. Since the sensitive boy likes to please his mom, she could simply tell her boy how much she appreciates it when he is behaving well and how she prefers it to his more contrary behaviors. Your son will respond in a positive manner when he is praised for cleaning up his toys rather than harshly reprimanded when he doesn't.

However, as with any child, it's important to delineate clear limits and expectations for your sensitive son. Mom should set limits in a calm yet firm manner. For example, you could tell your six-year-old son, "I hear that you would rather play with your toy car than put your coat on, but if you don't put on your coat now you'll be late for school. I know that you don't like walking into the classroom late, so let's make sure that when you come home from school there will be plenty of time to play with your favorite car." Remember that you are modeling appropriate boundary-setting behavior to your child.

It also helps when disciplining the sensitive boy to encourage him to express how he's feeling and to ask him to express what he wants. For instance, in the situation I just described, you could ask him to repeat, "I'm feeling frustrated since I want to play with my car instead of putting my coat on." When you praise him for verbalizing his feelings, you could also point out how much better it feels (for both of you) when he expresses himself rather than getting upset. This technique helps your son move from being overwhelmed by emotions to knowing how to manage them.

As we all know, no mom can be a full-time saint when her child is having a severe emotional meltdown. You should set your own boundaries by taking some time out for yourself if your son is having a temper tantrum. You may want to tell your son, "I love you. You are a wonderful boy, and I'm feeling upset right now. It would help both of us if we took a few minutes alone to calm down." Phrasing it this way will make it clear that the time out is not a punishment but rather a break for both of you. If taking time out to center yourself is not an option, you can mend the situation later. Once you realize that you overreacted, let your son know that you were feeling frustrated with his behavior and reassure him of your love and support. This admission will not only comfort and reassure your boy, but it will also let him know that parents are human too, and that everyone makes mistakes.

When you son is experiencing an intense reaction to physical stimulation, it would help to let your son know that the stimulation is temporary. For example, if your son is becoming very upset listening to a fire-engine siren going by your house, it would be helpful to say something like, "That noise really hurts your ears, and the painful sound will be over in a few seconds." When a child realizes that "this too shall pass," it will be easier for him to cope with the uncomfortable physical sensation. Also, hearing you acknowledge his experience lets him know that he is understood and that you can empathize with him.

In Elaine Aron's book *The Highly Sensitive Child*, she has succinctly summarized effective methods to discipline your sensitive child (2002). I strongly recommend that you read her suggestions for correcting the highly sensitive child.

How to Support Your Son

Every mother wants to support her child and help him become the best person he can be. There are some special challenges when mothering a highly sensitive boy, but a general attitude of understanding, compassion, and appreciation will go a long way toward smoothing the road ahead for each of you. Also, remembering to take care of yourself and having compassion for yourself when you make mistakes with your HSB will help you sustain yourself and be the best mother you can be to your HSB. Some specific guidelines to help you on your way are:

- Listen to your sensitive son and let him know that you acknowledge and accept his physical and emotional sensitivity.

- Help your son understand the causes for society's negativity toward sensitivity in males.

- Talk with your son about all of the positive aspects of being a sensitive boy and point out that sensitivity in males is admired in many cultures.

- Let your son know that everybody is different and that differences should be respected.

- Never tolerate anyone shaming your son's sensitivity. If you see that your boy is experiencing shame, try to counteract the feeling by gently pointing out the fallacy of the thinking behind it and letting your son know how wonderful you know he is.

- Tell your son about famous people and spiritual leaders who share his trait.

- If you accidentally criticize your son's sensitivity, quickly apologize and tell him that you made a mistake.

- Try to be vigilant about not putting your son into situations where he will be humiliated. Listen closely to his responses about activities and relationships and if he seems very uncomfortable in them, help him to remove himself from the situation.

- Ensure that your son feels safe in new situations. You can do this by sitting in on new activities to observe how it's going and also by listening closely to your son's responses about the situation. Remove him from environments that diminish his self-esteem.

- Show your son how to set personal boundaries with others.

- Frequently reassure your son that he always has your support and show him the truth of this statement by backing it up with actions.

Conclusion

Being a mother can be a tough job for any woman, and some might consider parenting a highly sensitive boy to be an especially hard challenge to face. However, it helps to remember that all children, sensitive or not, have characteristics or needs that require special attention and care. And, of course, the flip side of this dynamic is experiencing all the wonderful benefits of nurturing a sensitive boy: his loving nature, his creativity, his desire to please, and his ability to bond closely with you as his mom.

As you move through your days, try to remain centered in the feelings of love and devotion that you have for your child. Even when you feel frustrated or challenged by his sensitivity or his behavior, try to have compassion for both yourself and him in the situation. A gentle and calm approach toward both yourself and him will help you be the best mom you can be.

Next, we'll look at a father's role in bringing up his highly sensitive boy.

Chapter 3

When Dad Doesn't Connect to
His Sensitive Boy

"I really appreciated that my dad never forced me to get involved in activities that I didn't like and he took an interest in all my favorite hobbies. I think that his acceptance gave me a lot of self-confidence throughout my life."

"I was constantly told by my dad that I was too sensitive, and he would sometimes tease me about it. I remember once when I was watching a sad movie with my parents, I got teary-eyed and my dad started mocking me, telling me that real boys don't cry. Man, that really hurt."

In this chapter we will discuss how difficult it is for many dads to relate to a boy with a finely tuned nervous system and offer methods to help dads accept and enjoy their highly sensitive sons. But first we'll look at a father's role in raising his HSB and the all-too-common damage that can result when a father shames his sensitive boy.

The Father-Son Relationship

Most men remember incidents from their boyhood when their dad told them to "act like a man," especially when the child expressed fear or cried. While being shamed for expressing emotions is hurtful for the non-HSB, this reaction can be devastating for the sensitive boy. A boy longs for approval from his dad. He needs reassurance from this primary male role model that the boy is masculine enough, just as he is. So when a father shames a boy for expressing his genuine emotions, the boy's self-esteem plummets. The boy is given the message that he has to repress his true self to be accepted as a man.

Although some dads are now becoming more involved in their son's lives, most dads do not spend as much as much of their free time with their sons as moms do. One long-term research project that followed children from the time they were five years old through age thirty-one demonstrates that the most important influence on children was whether the father was involved in the child's care (Kindlon and Thompson, 1999). Fathers need to spend special, positive time with their sons. It doesn't matter what the activity is, as long as the father is available to and supportive of his son.

Dads treat their daughters differently than their sons. Research has shown that fathers treat their infant daughters more gently than they do baby boys. As the children grow up, fathers tend to show their sons less physical affection, correct them more often, and play more competitively with them. As the boy reaches adolescence, his father may begin to see him as competition. This attitude can result in a tendency for that father to control and criticize a son more than a daughter (Kindlon and Thompson, 1999). A dad who fails to actively support his sensitive son can create a deep emotional hurt or "father wound" that the boy may carry with him throughout life.

A Dad's Support Helps Raise the HSB's Self-Esteem

Dads have the vital role of teaching their sensitive sons how to deal appropriately with the aggressive boy culture. Many fathers erroneously believe that their sensitive sons should become more aggressive in order to fit in with the eighty percent non-HSBs. While a father does need to teach his son how to stand up for himself, he also has to understand, protect, and encourage his sensitive son (Aron, 2002). Both the father and the son benefit when that father accepts his son's trait of sensitivity instead of trying to mold him into a non-HSB. The dad will be able to relax and enjoy his relationship with his son, and the boy feels accepted and loved by his dad, giving him the confidence to assert himself with his more aggressive peers.

One of the few North American men in my study who was never teased as a child and never let others push him around was a man whose father totally supported him. Brian fondly remembered, "My dad loves to fight for the underdog, and he would always back me up if people put me down because I was sensitive. I remember him telling one of my elementary school teachers that she should be ashamed of herself for telling me I was strange when I preferred to read during recess rather than play outside. I also remember my dad telling me to be proud of my sensitive qualities. I think his unwavering support gave me a lot of confidence and the ability to believe in myself."

Dan mentioned how his father encouraged him to pursue his nontraditional interests: "My dad recognized when I was still young that my hobbies were different from my older brother's. I really appreciated that he didn't push me to play competitive sports, which I never enjoyed. My dad was sort of a renaissance man who enjoyed all sorts of activities. He passed down his passion for listening to classical music and reading the great masterpieces. We would spend many enjoyable hours listening to the great classical composers and discussing famous authors. I think this deep bond that I shared with my dad helped me to get over some of the rough times when I wasn't accepted by my peers in school."

An Inability to Connect

Most dads play with their sons in a rough-and-tumble manner. However, some sensitive boys may not enjoy physical play, finding it too overstimulating. Gary said, "I remember how scared I was of getting hurt when my dad played rough with me. I wanted to be held by my dad, not roughed up by him. But roughhousing was the only way he knew how to relate with me.

"My relationship with my father was not very good since he couldn't understand my sensitivity. He was an officer in the military, and I was brought up to believe that a real man should be able to handle any situation. I attended the Air Force Academy, which was supposed to mold me into this competent leader of men. I probably joined the Air Force to win my father's love and affection."

Many dads have a difficult time relating to or supporting their son when he pursues activities that are outside of the act-like-a-man box. Many HSMs told me how they had to deny their sensitivity to get their father's love and approval. Christian from Denmark told me, "My father tried to fulfill his dreams through me, and it turned out to be a disaster. I was a very shy boy, and my dad would pressure me to act more assertive at home and at school, telling me that men needed to seize the world. He wanted me to act like a Viking, yet I had anxiety just being in a group of other children."

Likewise, Jeffrey shared, "I wish my dad had recognized that there are different ways of being masculine. When I played clarinet in high school, my mom went to all my concerts, but my dad wouldn't come. Perhaps to get my dad's attention, I finally decided to go out for the soccer team, even though I really didn't like the sport. The only time my dad acknowledged me was when I played soccer, and he actually went to see me play on Saturdays. I guess I learned at a young age that I had to deny my real self to get my father's love."

Joel also had a dad who didn't support his sensitivity. "I was constantly told by my dad that I was too sensitive and he would sometimes tease me about it. I think my gentleness really threatened his sense of masculinity. I remember sitting at the dining room table with my parents and two brothers. I couldn't get a word in edgewise, so I got frustrated and started flapping my arms to get their attention. My dad started laughing at me, asking if I were a bird. He then got the entire family to laugh at me as I turned red with embarrassment and ran away from the table in tears. I still remember that incident to this day, and it still hurts."

Fathers would do well to let go of the cookie-cutter model of masculinity. Seeing your son as an individual, someone who will express his masculinity in his own way, will help you feel closer to your boy and help him thrive.

Alex is a father who is also highly sensitive. He and his fourteen-year-old sensitive son, Noah, were recently seen for counseling at their local family-service agency. Alex pushed Noah to go out for the football team even though Noah had no interest in that sport. Noah hated the way the coach treated him and finally quit going to practices. When Alex berated Noah for quitting the team, Alex's wife insisted that they see a family counselor.

Alex told the family therapist that he loathed weak men. Later during the counseling sessions, Alex admitted that Noah's gentle demeanor reminded him of how he was humiliated as a boy for his lack of aggression. Once Alex began attending family counseling sessions, he realized that he was forcing his son to deny his gentleness due to his internalized self-loathing for his own sensitivity. After several months of counseling, Alex finally began to be able to accept Noah—and himself— as the sensitive males that they are.

This kind of internalized negativity can be a common problem in fathers who are highly sensitive. They fear that their sons will have the negative experiences they suffered through as kids, and so they bend over backwards to try to force their sons to behave in a traditional masculine manner. Also, some fathers, sensitive or not, feel rejected when their highly sensitive sons decline to participate in "masculine" play. They see their efforts to roughhouse and model traditional masculinity to their boys as an act of love, and they become angry when those offers are not greeted with enthusiasm. In these cases, it's important for fathers to try to see past their own interpretation of events and begin to empathize with their boys. As the adult in the situation, it's incumbent on the father to support his son—not the other way around.

Male Role Models

Many HSMs in my study told me that it would have helped them if they had a role model of a sensitive man. Even if your son has a good relationship with his father, additional support is always helpful. Since most men either are not sensitive or repress their sensitivity, it may be difficult to find an HSM role model for your son. However, any compassionate older male who is supportive of your son will help raise his self-esteem. Are there are competent and trustworthy older males like uncles, grandfathers, relatives, neighbors, coaches, teachers, or counselors who could take a supportive role in your son's life? It's important that your son have positive experiences with both HSMs and non-HSMs to help prepare to interact with different types of men. For example, if you are a HSM dad who enjoys quiet, indoor activities, it may be beneficial for your son to occasionally spend time with a supportive compassionate, non-HSM high-sensation seeker who enjoys more stimulating activities. Likewise, if you are a non-HSM sensation seeker, it would be beneficial for your son to spend time with a considerate, sensitive man who prefers calm activities. Even a few positive experiences with a compassionate and supportive older male can raise your son's self-esteem and help him feel more secure in his masculinity. Seeing a variety of models can open your son's vistas, letting him see that there are many ways to be a successful, happy man.

Throughout my childhood I never had any adult male role models to encourage my athletic ability. Since I never knew how to play sports as a child and I was scared of joining in competitive games with aggressive boys, I would spend a lot of my boyhood alone in my room.

However, I clearly remember one wonderful exception to this rule. When I was five years old, some older boys whose parents were visiting my family went to play baseball in a nearby park and took me with them. One kind boy showed me how to hit the ball as we held the bat together. When we hit the ball, this compassionate boy showed me how to run around the bases as he yelled, "You hit a home run Teddy! Someday you're going to be a really good baseball player."

I recall how I joyfully ran after the baseball to retrieve the pop flies that were hit to the outfield on that glorious spring day. Even though I would later suffer humiliation in school due to my lack of self-confidence and the misperception that I lacked any athletic prowess, that one blissful incident stayed in my mind. Later, in my adolescence, the memory of that day probably gave me the confidence to go out for the high-school track team and encouraged me to become an avid basketball and baseball player as an adult.

Many HSMs who were raised in intergenerational extended families reported many positive experiences interacting with their older male relatives. For instance, even though Gary had a poor relationship with his dad who had difficulty accepting his sensitive son, he fondly remembered the support he received from his grandpa. "When I was eleven years old, I remember taking pictures of flowers on a hot summer afternoon with my grandpa. Although my dad never supported my interest in photography, Grandpa volunteered to help me take pictures. He held up a cardboard placard to block the direct sunlight, since the colors of the flowers were brighter in the shade than in the sun." Tears gathered in the corners of Gary's eyes as he reminisced about how loving his grandpa was to have stood in the sweltering sun to help him in his project.

Tom recalled, "When I was fourteen, my parents thought there was something wrong with me and sent me to a therapist who was a sensitive man. The therapist became a male role model for me, letting me know unequivocally that it was okay for me to be a sensitive boy. He probably saved my life by helping me learn to accept myself even though many people thought I was strange."

For many years I volunteered as a big brother for a branch of the Big Brothers/Big Sisters of America. When I first met Bill, he was a shy eight-year-old boy. He was reticent to play a game with me outside on the day we met, even though his mom and the representative from Big Brothers encouraged him to go outside with me. Bill wisely took his time to check me out before he felt safe enough to interact with me. As the months flew by, Bill's trust in me grew as we went on hikes, played basketball, or went boating at a nearby lake. I noticed that he had a difficult time handling overstimulation when I took him to an amusement park, so we tended to engage in less stimulating activities. Due to a job change, I relocated to a different town three hours away. After five years of weekly get-togethers, Bill and I didn't see each other anymore. Seven years after our Big Brother meetings ended, I was in Bill's hometown during Christmas week, and I decided to look him up. I was so pleased to see the centered, confident-looking, young college man in front of me, and I thought that perhaps some of my mentoring and support helped this previously shy, fearful boy grow into an emotionally well-adjusted, happy man.

Given all the publicity about children being exploited, it's crucial that parents carefully screen any potential male role model for their son. Even if the man has excellent references, the relationship may not help increase your son's self-esteem if the man doesn't know how to appropriately support your son. Parents should inform the male role model that their son is sensitive and give the mentor specific methods of how to interact with their HSB and activities that he enjoys.

Discipline by Dads

In my clinical experience, I've noticed that boys generally receive harsher discipline than girls by Dad including more frequent corporal punishment, which is particularly devastating to the sensitive boy. Hitting or harshly disciplining a sensitive boy is a shock to his nervous system that could possibly traumatize him. Remember Terry from Chapter Two? His older brother would just laugh in his mom's face when she screamed or slapped him, yet this kind of severe discipline devastated Terry. Dads need to be gentle when disciplining their sensitive boys.

While screaming and slapping are never effective disciplinary tactics, some aggressive boys may need very firm boundaries and stricter consequences. However, I can't emphasize enough that sensitive boys respond better to gentle discipline by both parents. As a dad, make sure that all the adults in your boy's life are consistent in administering mild discipline.

As I mentioned in the preceding chapter, since sensitive boys are responsible by nature and feel guilty when they make mistakes, corporal punishment and severe reprimands are not only unnecessary but will damage your son's self-esteem. As a father, it's important that you speak to your son in a gentle way to avoid frightening him. Aaron told me, "I wish that my dad had known that discipline didn't need to be as severe for me as for my brothers. A little correcting goes a long way with sensitive boys."

The sensitive boy is compassionate and doesn't want to hurt others, so Dad may just have to explain the consequences of his hurtful behavior for him to change. For example, if your son doesn't take out the garbage like he was supposed to, let him know that it will inconvenience you when you come home late from work. Set specific boundaries for your son and let him know in a calm manner the consequences of inappropriate behavior.

Dads Supporting their Sensitive Boys

All parents feel challenged by their responsibilities at times, and dads may have an especially tough time understanding and supporting a sensitive son. But there is much you can do to bond with your son and help him to grow into a strong and happy man. Let's take a look at some strategies that will help.

Learn a New Definition of Masculinity

Many fathers need to question their own beliefs about what it means to be a man and be open to looking at new definitions of masculinity. Dads need to be aware of how damaging it can be when aggressive male behavior is extolled in the media. For example, I recently picked up a book in my local bookstore about how fathers should raise their sons. I was alarmed to read, "Take your son to a hockey game. Boys love the fighting." While many boys enjoy aggressive, stimulating team activities, I don't think encouraging exposure to violence is ultimately helpful for any boy.

As the primary male role model in your son's life, it's important for you to stand courageously against the idea that a real man must be tough and unemotional. And, as a way to support and bond with your boy, you can discuss with him these notions of masculinity and how and why they exist. Presenting these roles as artificial cultural constructions will help your son see them as mutable and, ultimately, optional. And, if you'd like to explore these notions more yourself (perhaps so you can discuss the issue more clearly with your son), you can discuss the hazards and detrimental consequences of stereotypical male behavior with male friends, your wife, a counselor, in a men's group, or by reading such books as *The Wonder of Boys*, *Real Boys*, or *Raising Cain*.

As well as talking often with your son about the meaning of masculinity and what it really means to be a man, it will be helpful to reassure your sensitive boy that he doesn't need the approval of aggressive boys, athletes, or the alpha male to feel good about himself. It's also essential to frequently affirm your sensitive son's positive qualities.

Spending Quality Time with Your Son

Some dads (and moms) may find it difficult to slow down and concentrate on being present with their children. With everything a busy parent needs to do, sometimes dads find themselves on autopilot, coasting through their time with their sons. However, especially for fathers of highly sensitive sons, it's important to find the time and the enthusiasm to invest in your relationship with your boy. A sensitive child will sense when you're tuned out or not paying attention, and this will likely wound him. And by dedicating time to spend with your son, you will develop a richer, more enjoyable, and stronger relationship with him.

Ideally, a dad will become very involved with his new child during his wife's pregnancy and will bond with the newborn once he arrives.

As your son grows, dedicate yourself to frequently showing your gentle, sensitive side, which will model this behavior for your son and will build trust and love between you. Since dads tend to play with their young sons in a more stimulating manner than with daughters, be on the lookout for signs of overstimulation in your son. For example, the overstimulated toddler will show signs of distress or may turn his ahead away when overaroused. At that moment, Dad should quiet down and gently caress his son.

Like Dan, whose dad spent countless hours with him listening to music and discussing books, find out what activities your son enjoys and participate in the boy's hobbies. Another option is to encourage your son to go on adventures with you, as long as he feels comfortable engaging in the activity. Never shame your son if he doesn't feel comfortable participating in the venture. Regardless of the activity, a dad needs to interact with an HSB in a gentle, respectful manner, which will increase the boy's self-esteem (Aron, 2002).

There are plenty of calm activities that a dad and his son can do together. If you're interested in sports, your son may prefer to watch a quiet sporting event like tennis or golf, where even the commentators talk in soft voices. However, every boy is different, and in the chapter on boys and sports, we will meet sensitive men who enjoyed hockey, football, and hunting as boys. Don't hesitate to offer to play a sport or attend any athletic event with your son as long as he doesn't feel that he should engage in the sport to please you.

It's beneficial for dad and son to participate in an activity without always including the entire family. Your son will get individual attention and encouragement from you, and the sensitive boy generally does better in a quiet, one-on-one environment. Joel recalled, "It was a disaster when dad would take my brothers and me to play miniature golf since I used to feel rotten when I played poorly. I couldn't concentrate when everyone was watching me hit the ball. All of us kids ended up screaming at each other as we accused each other of cheating, yet I was the one who used to frequently end up getting punished. How I longed for special time alone with my dad. Unfortunately, it never happened, since dad believed we should always do things together as a family."

Since sensitive boys are naturally compassionate and concerned about the welfare of people, animals, and the environment, an excellent father/son activity is to get involved in service projects such as serving food at a soup kitchen, volunteering at an animal shelter, or planting trees. Not only will you be raising your son's self-esteem by spending quality time with him, but you will be helping uplift society.

Be a Strong, Sensitive Dad

Make sure that you always defend your son if others shame his sensitivity. Frequently praise your son's sensitive attributes, and let him know that you really understand him. Model setting limits with others so that he will learn how to set boundaries if he is humiliated for his sensitivity.

As the most important male role model for his son, a dad needs to express his feelings as well as be able to show his vulnerability. Be like Rosy Grier, the former NFL football player, who sang on the 1970s record album *Free to Be You and Me*, " It's all right to cry little boy, I know some big boys that cry too" (Thomas, 1972). When you express your full range of emotions, you will be setting an example for your son that a real man can be a fully functioning human being. Rather than living in that act-like-a-man box, be a model for your son of the diversity of masculinity, including the "softer side" of being a man.

Conclusion

In this chapter we explored the unique relationship of a highly sensitive son and his father. As primary role models for their sons, many fathers feel a great deal of pressure to mold their sons into the traditional western male model of toughness, aggression, and limited emotional expression. Dads often respond to this pressure by encouraging their sons to participate in rough athletic play with other boys and discouraging any demonstration of emotion. In the most painful cases, some dads actively shame their sons when these boys don't conform to the powerful stereotype of masculinity. Adults may do this because they feel afraid that their boys won't fit in and be successful unless they conform with traditional norms, or the dads in question may actually be projecting a self-loathing that they developed as young boys when they were shamed and humiliated for their sensitivity.

As a father, it will be most helpful for you and your son if you try to separate your fears and negative feelings from your interactions with your HSB. Express the deep love you feel for your son by accepting him unconditionally, participating with him in activities he enjoys, and modeling for him a strong, sensitive, and inclusive masculinity that he can be comfortable with.

Next, we'll be looking at the HSB's experience in school.

Chapter 4

The Sensitive Boy at School

"A lot of my memories of school are unpleasant since I never really felt like I fit in with the other kids. However, in second grade I had a really nice teacher who encouraged me academically. Thanks to Mrs. Mabry's support, I actually enjoyed going to school, since I was proud of myself for always getting the top grades in my class."

"Even though my parents understood my sensitivity, school was a nightmare for me. Some of the teachers were downright mean and humiliated me in front of the class when I had trouble answering their questions. It's still painful to think of those shaming experiences by my insensitive teachers."

In this chapter we will discuss the special challenges for the sensitive boy attending a public school. The HSB can thrive in a public school, but he may need some special attention and support to make the most of this experience. We'll also look at why the HSB is susceptible to bullying in school and ways to prevent your son from being bullied. Finally, I'll offer some innovative methods to help you create a positive environment for the sensitive boy in school, and we'll look at alternatives to public schools that may serve your boy better.

Public School and the Sensitive Boy

As you know, most children aren't as susceptible to overstimulation as is the highly sensitive child. This means that the common public school classroom can be exceedingly challenging for the HSB. Since eighty percent of the children in a public-school class are not highly sensitive, teachers are not trained to take sensitivity into consideration and may not know how to recognize it. This can leave the HSB without the support he needs to do his best in school.

Frequently, the sensitive boy feels overwhelmed in a large public-school classroom with its stimulation, bright overhead fluorescent lights, and the pressure to perform well. Many HSBs have a particularly difficult time learning in a noisy environment. I remember when I was a substitute teacher in a public elementary classroom many years ago. All the fourth-grade classes were in the same large room, separated by flimsy dividers. I could hear a cacophony of many sounds emanating from the different classrooms and could barely concentrate on teaching my students. Parents should spend time in their son's classroom to evaluate how conducive the environment is for his academic progress and social adjustment. If the classroom is too overstimulating, you should work with the teacher and school administration to reduce stimulation.

Many sensitive boys feel anxious, alienated, and alone in school since they don't fit in with the eighty percent nonsensitive children. Research by Elaine Aron found that by school age, most sensitive boys are introverts, perhaps since society has given them a message that there is something wrong with them. Therefore, sensitive boys become cautious in group settings, pausing to observe how they will be treated. In Michael Gurian's book *The Mind of Boys*, he describes a school social worker who worked with sensitive boys and found that those students yearned for attachment and love in a school environment they considered hostile to them.

Sensitive students usually work differently from their counterparts. They pick up on subtle cues in the environment and have difficulty learning when they are overaroused. If a sensitive student is not contributing much to a discussion, it doesn't necessarily mean that he doesn't understand the material or isn't paying attention. Sensitive boys frequently are shy about speaking up, and they like to pause to reflect about the subject matter before speaking.

Lars, a psychologist from Denmark, noted, "I was very shy and embarrassed to make mistakes in front of my classmates so I avoided speaking up spontaneously in class which made me feel more uncomfortable. I would always try to figure out what was the right thing to say before speaking up. This hesitance made the teachers think I didn't understand the material, and they would be surprised when I earned consistently high grades throughout school."

Unsupportive Teachers and the Sensitive Boy

Many teachers think there is something wrong with a boy who pauses to observe, since they may believe the myth that all boys should be aggressive sensation seekers (Aron, 2002). Some teachers rigidly promote stereotypical boy behavior, even in young boys. Steve told me that he remembered being very shy and scared upon entering his first-grade classroom on the first day of school. He recalled feeling so overjoyed to see his friend enter the same class that he ran over and hugged him. However, his ignorant teacher sent both Steve and his friend to the office for inappropriate sexual behavior. Instead of chastising shy, sensitive boys, teachers need to learn to appreciate their special qualities. Sensitive boys rarely fight, bully, lie, or create disruptive behavior in school.

Many teachers subscribe to the false belief that boys need to be treated rougher and punished in a stronger manner than girls. They don't realize that twenty percent of the boys in their class are sensitive and that severe discipline can be counterproductive and possibly traumatic for them. For instance, when I was in third grade, my teacher put me in the "bad" row with two other students who didn't conform to the classroom rules. As a creative, sensitive boy, I would get bored with the formal lessons and would sometimes walk around the room. The stigma of being labeled bad for being curious severely lowered my academic self-confidence. Teachers need to be informed that inquisitive, sensitive boys should be given creative outlets, rather than being ostracized and punished.

Even one humiliating experience by a teacher could damage a sensitive boy's entire scholastic career. Tom remembered, "I was very shy as a boy and afraid to speak up in class. Although I never felt comfortable in school, up until the fourth grade I got pretty good grades. However I was devastated when my fourth-grade teacher told me in front of the entire class that there was something wrong with me for not answering her questions. I think she had it in for me. She would constantly call on me even though she knew that I got nervous about speaking in front of the class. That dreadful experience affected the way I felt about going to school. Around that time I developed what they call 'school phobia,' and from fourth grade on my grades suffered."

Even though Jeffrey had a supportive mother, his teacher's cruel behavior had a devastating impact on him. He reported, "When I was in fifth grade I told my mom that some of the other children were teasing me. My mom spoke to my teacher, Ms. Greer, about the problem. The following day, Ms. Greer stood up in front of the class and told the other students that my mom had complained that children were making fun of me, saying that I had peed in my pants. That sadistic teacher began laughing and said, 'It's not nice to say Jeffrey peed in his pants.' Naturally, all the other children began laughing hysterically as I blushed with shame and embarrassment, trying to hold back tears. After that incident, the teasing became worse, and even my mom couldn't help me. I think that's when all my problems in school began."

Parents need to critically evaluate how their son's teacher treats him by regularly discussing with his teacher how he's doing, talking to other parents, and volunteering in the classroom. If you find out that a teacher is mistreating your son, you need to immediately let the teacher and principal know that their behavior is unacceptable. If the teacher is not receptive to changing his or her behavior, you should not let your son remain in the classroom.

You may recall that in the preceding chapter, I presented Brain's story about his father's supportive attitude. With the self-confidence his father helped to instill in him, Brian had the confidence to prevent other kids from pushing him around. When Brian's teacher put Brian down for reading during recess instead of playing, his dad told that teacher that she should be ashamed of herself for humiliating his son. Likewise, the adults in a sensitive boy's life need to unequivocally support their son in the face of a teacher's mistreatment.

Teachers and School Personnel Helping the HSB

Most boys have difficulty verbalizing their feelings, even sensitive boys. However, there are innovative methods teachers can use with HSBs (and non-HSBs) when a boy gets upset. As author Michael Gurian puts it, "Physical-kinesthetic activity (like bouncing a ball) helps boys develop their brain toward emotional communication through words and actions. Spatial-physical activity (especially physical movement) helps promote emotional safety and emotional communication in boys. Boys feel safe and have an easier time accessing emotions when the teacher (or any adult) is doing something with him" (2007).

In his book *The Minds of Boys*, Gurian describes a fifth-grade teacher working with a sensitive boy in her class. This HSB would run out of the classroom whenever he got upset. The boy had difficulty managing his sensitivity to stimuli in the large classroom, yet he wouldn't talk about his problems when the teacher tried to help him. One day the teacher tried bouncing a ball back and forth with the boy as she spoke to him. This worked wonderfully, as the physical activity took some of the pressure off of the situation, allowing the boy the safety and space to express his emotions until he had calmed down enough to return to the classroom. For the rest of the year the boy was able to ask for help when an adult teacher or staff would bounce a ball with him.

A sensitive boy may need increased one-to-one bonding with his teacher in order to feel emotionally safe in the classroom. Jay, who was raised in New Britain, Connecticut, told me how a compassionate teacher helped him feel safe when he was in fourth grade. "Mrs.

Whitlaw sometimes used to let me help her clean the classroom during recess. I felt like I was special, getting to clean the blackboard and straighten the chairs. One day she told me that she noticed how sad I looked walking around the playground by myself when I went outside during recess. I guess I felt safe with her. I remember telling her that the other boys didn't want to play with me since I wasn't any good at football or dodge ball, and those games are all the other boys wanted to play. I told Mrs. Whitlaw about the time I played hopscotch with the girls. All the other boys teased me, calling me a girl, so I didn't want to go outside during recess.

"Mrs. Whitlaw told me that she liked gentle boys and that the world could use a lot more helpful boys like me. She told me that the other children were wrong for making fun of me. Later, Mrs. Whitlaw began praising me in front of the class, saying how helpful and kind I was. I think this helped make the other kids like me, which made me feel better about myself. Mrs. Whitlaw was the only teacher who praised me for being sensitive when I was a child." If there were more teachers like Mrs. Whitlaw, sensitive boys would have an easier time navigating through the aggressive public-school environment. Later in this chapter I'll offer specific methods to help you inform teachers how to best work with your son.

How Teachers Treat HSBs in Different Cultures

According to researchers Charles Super and Sarah Harkness, the over-stimulating public-school classroom is more prevalent in American schools than European schools, which tend to be more orderly and calm (Harkness, 2000). The HSMs from Thailand and India and most of the men from Denmark reported that their teachers treated them with respect and kindness. This is in stark contrast to many of the HSMs who attended public school in North America and reported that teachers frequently shamed them for their sensitivity.

Tun, who grew up in Thailand, recalled, "Although you couldn't really question the teachers like they do in America, the students were very respectful toward them. In turn, the teachers treated the students in a kind manner."

Ashok told me, "Growing up in India, I felt supported and loved by my teachers. One of the reasons why I enjoyed school is that I knew that my teachers really cared about me. In India we have a deep respect for teachers and would never want to offend them."

Hans' experiences in Denmark were typical of most of the Danish HSMs. "My teachers recognized my positive attributes as a sensitive boy. I think they appreciated my serious and mature attitude in school. Their recognition of my good qualities built up my self-confidence."

Some of the North American teachers also appreciated that their sensitive boys were good students. Alan mentioned, "I grew up in Pittsburgh and my teachers were supportive of me since I was often the smartest kid in the class. The teachers liked that I followed the rules and behaved myself."

My study showed that, generally, HSMs from India, Thailand, and Denmark didn't experience as much shaming from teachers as they were growing up. While North American HSBs may be more vulnerable to judgment from teachers who are ignorant about sensitivity, some men, like Alan, did have positive experiences with his American teachers. Alan's experiences show that North America teachers can learn how to treat sensitive boys in a compassionate and supportive manner.

School Bullies and the Sensitive Boy

The school bully is now a widely recognized scourge, terrorizing schools with his or her cruel and sometimes violent behavior. And, since bullies tend to target kids who seem different from others, HSBs are particularly vulnerable to bullying in school. However, this targeting of perceived differences isn't reserved for the sensitive kids. For instance, a 1991 study conducted by S. Ziegler and M. Rosenstein-Mannon found that thirty-eight percent of students involved in special education were bullied compared to eighteen percent of other students (Carpenter, 2009). Beginning around age ten, a boy's peer group demands conformity. Anything a boy does that's different is usually used to ridicule him.

According to Swedish researcher Dan Olweos, one of the main characteristics of victims of bullies is that they are reluctant to defend themselves or retaliate (Carpenter, 2009). Sadly, boys must be willing to fight to prove their manliness amongst other males or they risk being humiliated. Yet eighty-five percent of the HSMs in my survey said that they always avoided fighting when they were boys. This resistance to participate in what is seen as normal male violence may be the prime factor why so many sensitive boys are bullied.

Sensitive boys react more strongly to most events than do other boys. This tendency adds to their vulnerability, as bullies strive to get a reaction from their victims. More reaction, more bullying. So when a bully sees that the HSB gets visibly upset in response to bullying, the bully is likely to intensify the abuse. Interestingly, physical characteristics such as weight, height, or wearing glasses are not correlated with being bullied. Therefore, even a short, skinny boy wearing thick glasses who doesn't react to a bully and fights back will rarely be harassed.

Bullying in North American Schools

Bullies can take the fun out of school and turn something simple like a ride on the school bus, a stop at a locker, or a walk to the bathroom into a scary event that's anticipated with worry all day. According to the National Association of School Psychologists 160,000 children miss school every day in the United States for fear of being bullied (Pollack, 1999).

Although sensitive boys are particularly vulnerable to being bullied, they are usually not willing to ask an adult for help. This reluctance may be because they feel embarrassed about being victimized, afraid of further retaliation, or hopeless about what the adult can do to help. In the saddest cases, HSBs may not report abuse because they believe that they deserve the humiliation. Research indicates that many bullied children experience learning difficulties, becoming so anxious to avoid bullying that they lose their ability to concentrate in the classroom. Children who are bullied experience low self-esteem, anxiety and depression (Nansel et al., 2001).

Illustrating the devastating effect that bullying has on sensitive boys, some of the HSMs I spoke to shared some horrific stories of being bullied in the United States. Terry, who was raised in the New York area, told me that his years in middle school were a living nightmare. "Not one teacher or my parents had a clue how I was being physically and verbally assaulted daily. As a very thin, nonathletic, fearful boy, I lacked the self-confidence to fight back. When I reached middle school, other boys began punching me. It was like dodging bullets trying to make it between classes without getting severely bruised.

"The most dangerous area for me to venture into was the basement locker room before and after gym class. I was a target for the most vicious bullies as I tried to avoid getting constantly punched. One huge, muscular boy was called Lou, and he must have outweighed me by seventy-five pounds. Lou sadistically enjoyed punching me as hard as he could. Perhaps my deep fear of violence or getting severely hurt contributed to my not wanting to fight back.

"At any rate, I began having problems falling asleep at night as I dreaded being tortured at school the next day, and I was no longer able to focus on my schoolwork. However, I was too embarrassed to tell my parents—not that they could have done anything to help me anyway. They used to just get upset with me for getting bad grades. How could I listen to a teacher when the guy in the seat behind me was smashing me on my head with his knuckles, telling me how he was going to beat me up in the hallway when the bell rang? I remember once, in math class, one boy behind me kept smacking me in the back of my head. I got so upset that I began nervously banging my pencil on the desk. The teacher angrily stopped the math lesson and began screaming at me for distracting the class."

No child should ever have to go through the emotional and physical pain that Terry experienced. Since, like Terry, your son may be embarrassed to tell you that he is being bullied in school, it's crucial for parents, teachers, extended-family members, and friends to be vigilant in looking for and recognizing the signs that your son may be bullied.

Signs that Your Son Is Being Bullied

The following signs may indicate that your HSB is being bullied:

- Bumps and bruises
- The invention of mysterious illnesses to avoid school
- Belongings or money missing
- Sleep problems
- Irritability
- Depression
- Poor concentration
- Unexpected changes in routine
- Problems with schoolwork

Solutions to Bullying

It can be devastating for parents to discover that their child is a victim of bullying. It may bring back painful memories of the abuse the parents experienced in their school days. At the very least, knowing that someone you love so very much is being terrorized, hurt, and humiliated can cause a parent to feel helpless, angry, and very distressed.

However, there are tactics you can teach your child that will help him avoid or overcome bullying. The following are some practical solutions that you can help your son implement to cope with bullies.

Act brave, walk away, and ignore the bully. Tell your son to look the bully in the eye and say something like, "If you can't talk to me in a respectful way, I don't want you to talk to me. I'm giving you fair warning: back off now." You can role-play with your son using different scenarios. Counsel him to then walk away and ignore any further taunts. Encourage him to "walk tall" and hold his head up high (using this type of body language sends a message that your son isn't vulnerable). Bullies thrive on the reaction they get, so walking away from or ignoring the bully denies him the charge he's seeking. A bully who is ignored will probably get bored with trying to bother your son. Bullies want to know they have control over your son's emotions. Each time they get a reaction from him, it adds fuel to the bully's behavior.

Use humor. In a situation where your son has to deal with a bully and can't walk away with poise, tell him to use humor or offer a compliment to throw the bully off guard such as saying, "Hey, cool shoes you're wearing, dude."

Tell an adult. If your son is being bullied, emphasize that it's very important for him to tell an adult. Teachers, principals, and lunchroom personnel at school can all help to stop the abuse. Studies show that schools where principals crack down on this type of behavior have less bullying (Carpenter, 2009).

Use the buddy system. Encourage your son to enlist the help of a friend or a group that can help him (and perhaps others) to stand up to bullies. The bully wants attention—to be recognized and feel powerful—so a lot of bullying happens in the presence of peers. If the other kids in the group reject the bully's behavior, the bully won't get the reaction he or she seeks and will most likely stop the behavior.

Develop more friendships by joining social organizations, clubs, or sports programs. Encourage regular play or social visits with other children. Being in a group with other kids may help to build your son's self-esteem and give him a larger group of positive peers to spend time with and turn to.

Have your son learn self-defense. Knowing that he can defend himself if needed will give your HSB the self-confidence to stand up to a bully. In the following chapter on boys and sports, we'll look at more positive results of teaching the sensitive boy self-defense.

Discussing Bullying with Your Son

When you try to broach the subject of your son's experience with bullies, he may understandably become very upset. It may be very soothing to your boy to connect physically with him while talking, such as putting your hand on his shoulder. However, you need to be respectful of his space if he is the type of boy who doesn't want to be touched. The subject of bullying may bring up feelings of fear, embarrassment, shame, and anger in your HSB, so it's important that you behave with maturity, calmness, and compassion when talking about your son's experience. Learning that your son is being bullied may likely trigger an emotional reaction in you, but try to remember to focus on your son's experience rather than yours. Behaving in an angry way while discussing bullying will probably add to your son's burden in the situation, as he may likely believe that your painful emotions are his fault. So, though you may be boiling inside, try to avoid acting in a way that shows those feelings. Your boy will want to know that you can help him solve this problem, not get swept away by it as he is.

Be sure to validate your son's feelings and reassure him that he isn't to blame. Explain that bullies are often confused or unhappy people who don't feel good about themselves, and that bullying is wrong and cruel behavior. The key to helping your son deal with bullying is to help him regain a sense of dignity and recover damaged self-esteem (Gurian, 2005). Supporting him and clarifying that the situation stems from the bully's shortcomings—not your son's—can help him regain his emotional footing.

Tom remembered one cold Sunday afternoon in January when his parents asked him if he was being bullied in school. "I guess my parents noticed that something was bothering me at home since I would always mope around the house and easily get angry. When I was in seventh grade, there was one nasty kid in my class who suddenly started teasing me every day. I couldn't stand it.

"I vividly remember my dad sitting on the bed next to me in my bedroom asking me if anyone in school was teasing me. I felt deep embarrassment and kept rigidly denying it, until I broke down crying.

My dad rarely paid any attention to me, but he was there for me that day. He comforted me and let me know that I had his support. He didn't do a perfect job—I mean, he suggested that I invite the bully over so I could beat him at ping-pong (I was really good at the game). But the feeling of support he gave me in the situation was invaluable. Even though the bully kept teasing me, it didn't bother me as much since I wasn't hiding the shame and I had the support of my parents." Following this example, you can let your son know that you will always be available and open to anything he wants to discuss, including things that happen at school. Knowing that he has your support and love will help your son feel safe in coming to you with his problems.

If your son has tried the methods I mentioned above but the bullying does not stop (or becomes violent), go ahead and contact your son's school. Your son's safety and sense of well-being is of prime importance, so you have every justification to bring the issue to his teacher, school counselor, and/or principal. You may even consider talking to the bully's parents. However, before you contact other adults it's important that you have accurate documentation and witnesses if possible. For instance, you could have your son write down the date and time of the incident and what transpired. It would be helpful to find another student who witnessed the event and can corroborate your son's story. If your son's physical safety is in jeopardy and the school authorities won't intervene, you could contact the police. However, it may be more prudent to remove your son from a potentially physically violent situation if the bullying escalates to that point.

You could ask the P.T.A. or the principal to arrange for a professional to come to the school to offer an anti-bullying program. Parents and educators need to teach children that cruelty can never be tolerated or ignored. The culture of boy cruelty imposes a code of silence on boys requiring that boys don't speak up when they or others are being abused. Boys need to be taught that going along with a taunting crowd is a sign of weakness and that it takes a strong young man to speak up when he sees injustice.

Cross-Cultural Research on Bullying

According to my research, sensitive boys in Asian countries like Thailand and India don't seem to experience the same kind of malicious bullying as do HSBs who grow up in North America. Nui from Thailand told me, "Even though I was more sensitive than the other boys in my class, no one ever teased me. At my school I never saw anyone bully other children. Even when one of the boys teased another, it was done in fun and no one felt hurt."

Even though some HSMs from Denmark felt that they weren't as popular as the more assertive boys in school, none of the interviewees stated that they were viciously bullied like Terry was in the United States. As I quoted Hans earlier, "Denmark is a consensus culture, and the Danes usually don't like very aggressive behavior." However, according to an e-mail from Danish HSP therapists Martin and Lise August, "Even though Danish society is less aggressive than the United States, a subtle 'masculine code' still exists that can be challenging for Danish sensitive males" (October 10, 2009).

Making Positive Changes in Your Son's School

Look for practical ways to support your sensitive boy in school. For instance, volunteering in your son's classroom will help you better determine if your boy's needs are being met. Meeting with your son's teacher can be tremendously helpful, as you can help him or her better understand your son's sensitivity. Let the teacher know in a non-confrontational manner that your son has a trait whereby he prefers to observe and reflect before acting, compared to most boys who tend to act quickly and take risks. Remind the teacher that while both strategies succeed in some situations and fail in others, boys are generally expected to be decisive risk-takers. Let his teacher know that these cultural mores only serves to lower the self-esteem of the sensitive boy (Aron, 2002) and ask for help in supporting your son and helping him succeed in school.

If reaching out to your son's teacher doesn't seem to help, you can also meet with the school counselor and/or the principal. Don't be reticent about taking your concerns where you need to in order to get more of the results you're looking for. If your son's teacher proves to be unwilling to support your son (and especially if he or she is disrespectful to your child), you may want to discuss with the school principal the possibility of him changing classes. And, before the next school year, be sure to meet with school officials to determine which classroom would best support your son for the coming year.

Taking these steps will not only help your son on a practical level (getting him the scholastic and social support he needs in school), but it will help you feel empowered and will let your son know in a very concrete way that you are in his corner.

Tips for Teachers Working with Sensitive Children

When you meet with your son's teacher to discuss his trait of sensitivity, let her know the following points (Aron, 2002):

1. Every class will have approximately twenty percent highly sensitive children.

2. You will be happy to work closely with him or her to share insight on how to best work with your son.

3. Since sensitive children are creative, your boy will learn more effectively with creative approaches to lessons. Offer examples of what you mean, and express a willingness to make suggestions.

4. Your son doesn't learn well when he is overstimulated, so it will be helpful to create a calm classroom. He will perform better when he is relaxed.

5. Sensitive children like to observe before joining in new situations, so it would work best to let your son join in at his own rate.

6. Your son performs better when he is not being closely observed.

7. Let your son know in advance of any changes in the classroom, such as a change in the seating arrangement.

8. Recognize that some inappropriate behavior may be due to over-stimulation and never use harsh discipline with him.

9. Try to help your son with any social problems that you notice, like helping him make friends. For example, the teacher can encourage friendship by having your HSB work on a project with a friendly child. Your son will thrive with one good friend.

10. Encourage your son in his exceptional abilities.

11. Your son will benefit greatly from positive adult mentoring.

12. Be accepting and supportive if your son does not want to join in rough-and-tumble games with other boys. Emphasize to the other students that everyone has different abilities and interests and that these differences need to be respected.

Other Options to Attending a Public School

If, after trying to make positive changes for your son in his public school environment, he is still having a difficult time, you may want to consider other options. The bottom line is that your son should never be in an academic environment where his self-esteem suffers.

Alternative Schools

There are many alternative schools such as Montessori, Steiner, and local progressive, private schools that may be more conducive to your son's emotional and educational needs than a large public school. However, be aware that some alternative schools can be just as noisy as a public-school classroom. One HSM, Ryan, reported that although he went to a progressive elementary school, he found it difficult to learn with other children constantly talking and running around the class all the time.

For several years I worked at a small alternative school, The San Francisco Mobile School, for children from sixth to tenth grade. While the school offered an incredibly enriching experience for all the students, I noticed that some of the sensitive children had difficulty constantly traveling and interacting 24/7 with others during the many long trips the school promoted. When choosing an alternative school for your son, it's vital to evaluate the level of stimulation at the school and the staff's willingness to work with your son's temperament.

If your son attends a small, nurturing alternative elementary school and then plans to go to a large public school afterwards, he will have to learn how to cope with the institutionalized public school environment. It could be quite traumatic for your son to suddenly begin attending a crowded public classroom. My son, Dave, who was not a highly sensitive boy, still found it extremely challenging going from a small private middle school to a large public high school.

Al attended a small, supportive private school in San Francisco from kindergarten through fifth grade. Whenever there was a problem between students, the teacher would sit down with both students and work out the disagreement in a loving and respectful manner. Al had never been exposed to the cruel boy culture. Since the school only went up to fifth grade and his mom, Caroline, could not find a similar alternative middle school, Al began attending his local, urban middle school. When he began attending the large public school in sixth grade, it was a traumatic for Al to be exposed to the aggressive and overstimulating environment. He was overwhelmed by the aggressive boys, noise, and the rigid teachers at the sterile institution. The tough, big-city school was too much for Al's sensitive nervous system, and after a few months Caroline decided to homeschool him.

Homeschooling Your Son

If you're unable to find a school that can create a calm, supportive environment for your son, you may want to consider homeschooling your child. To compensate for the lack of social interaction, it's important for your son to get together with other children who are also being homeschooled and to enroll him in special classes. While some parents may have concerns about whether homeschooling is a good option for their child, for certain sensitive boys it would be better than having your son attend a school that lowers his self-worth. No sensitive boy should have to suffer in school like some of the HSMs in my study did, which left them with permanent emotional scars.

There are many different ways to homeschool your son. If you decide to homeschool, you need to make sufficient time for teaching and be comfortable with the dual role of parent and teacher. Before you decide to become your son's teacher, you should deeply consider if you have the emotional temperament to work with your son throughout the day.

I regret how easily I became frustrated when I tried to tutor my son in Spanish many years ago, and in retrospect, I wish I had hired someone else to tutor him. If you don't feel prepared to become your son's full-time teacher, consider these alternative options:

- Your school district may have a charter school where homeschooled children meet regularly with certified teachers.

- You could create a cooperative with other parents who are homeschooling their children and share the teaching assignments.

- You can organize educational outings with other parents of children being homeschooled.

- Your teenage son could possibly take courses at your local junior college or attend an internship working with another adult.

- You could hire tutors for your son.

Homeschooling is ideal for most sensitive boys since the HSB thrives in a safe, quiet, less-stimulating environment where they are free to pursue both core and creative subjects at their own pace. Pamela, a mom from San Diego, found that her sensitive son, Troy, became less anxious once he left his public school classroom at ten years old. Pamela reported, "Troy felt confined with the rigid daily lesson plans that his teacher demanded all the students follow. My son has always been musically inclined, and since he's been homeschooled he spends several hours a day playing the piano and the guitar. I noticed that since Troy wasn't disturbed by classroom overstimulation, he was able to learn the basics like reading, math, and history faster than when he was in a noisy public school classroom.

"I feel that sensitive children who are homeschooled are healthier emotionally than those who have to endure the conformity, rigidity, and intensity of a public school. This is Troy's sixth year being home-schooled, and now that he's sixteen, he's enrolled in two classes at a local junior college, where he's flourishing."

As I mentioned, the HSB who is being homeschooled should definitely attend different activities and classes, possibly with other homeschooled children. In addition, it would also be beneficial for him to learn how to navigate through the majority non-HSB culture by his attending after-school group activities. I know a young man named Connor, a thirteen-year-old from Portland, Oregon, who has been homeschooled his entire life. His parents have always enrolled him in community after-school activities so that he would learn how to interact with other children and make new friends. When he first began playing on his local Little League baseball team several years ago, Connor didn't play as aggressively as the other boys. He felt as though he didn't fit in and became quite discouraged. However, with the support of his parents and coach he quickly learned how to play more forcefully and became well-integrated into the team, ending up being one of the star players. This experience— the awkwardness followed by success—let him know that he was supported and valuable, which really increased his self-esteem.

Conclusion

As we've seen, school can be a difficult environment for the highly sensitive boy. As a prime socializing agent, school is often the place where the HSB begins to feel that he is different and not a "real" boy. And, when in the classroom environment, the noisy, intense, and sometimes disorganized atmosphere can trigger a great deal of anxiety and distraction for the HSB. School is also usually the first place where a child experiences bullying, which can be a truly damaging phenomenon.

However, there are plenty of options you can utilize to help make your son's educational experience a positive and enriching one. Try to remember that, as a parent, you are empowered to work with your son's school to improve the environment for your HSB. And, if the public-school environment remains a bad fit, you can try alternative schools or teach him at home. There are also options available to help deal with bullying, including talking with school staff, teaching your son strategies to avoid or dissuade bullies, and helping his confidence and self-efficacy with self-defense classes.

As in most of the chapters in this book, the bottom line remains the importance of understanding and supporting your HSB. The more you participate in your son's life and show your support for him, the deeper and richer your relationship will be and the more secure your son will eventually feel.

Our next chapter looks at the peer relationships of the HSB and the ways you can support your son in making lasting bonds outside the home.

Chapter 5

Making and Keeping Friends

"*I always felt anxious hanging out with the guys in my neighborhood since I knew that I couldn't match their daring behavior. I remember once when I was afraid to jump off a rope swing, the other guys laughed at me and called me a wimp and baby girl. I remember feeling emotionally devastated that day.*"

"*My mom encouraged me to hang out with the more studious kids in school, which was actually quite a relief. The academically advanced group treated each other more respectfully than most kids.*"

In this chapter, we'll look at the unique challenges and opportunities facing the highly sensitive boy in making social ties. HSBs play and interact differently than most other boys, which can cause problems when they seek to reach out socially. However, the HSB's sensitivity and tendency to select single "best" friends can make them a dependable friend of true value, the kind of friend we'd all like to have.

Running with the Pack

Most boys prefer to socialize in large groups, while many girls prefer dyads and triads. In large groups, boys can focus on a task, feel powerful, feel part of a collective and not feel invaded by emotional stimulation (Gurian, 1996). This tendency stands in stark contrast to the social habits of the sensitive boy, who has a natural tendency to pause to reflect before engaging in a task and may feel overwhelmed in group situations. Unlike most boys, sensitive boys usually prefer to interact with only one friend or play by themselves rather than interacting with a large group of boys. Ninety percent of the HSMs in my survey responded that, as kids, they "usually" or "always" played by themselves or with just one friend.

However, according to Michael Gurian, "Boys need to compete and do combat; they need to feel tested in the physical and interpersonal world. Encoded in the boys' brains are millions of years of the tribal experience of hunters" (1996). Gurian is speaking of the majority of boys, and the needs he speaks of aren't really relevant for most HSBs. Since they shy away from aggressive, combative interactions, HSBs may have difficulties making friends with other boys. My initial research indicated that most sensitive boys tended to avoid combative and competitive situations. Given this disparity between how the HSB and non-HSB behave, it's not surprising that ninety percent of the HSMs I've studied told me that they felt like they didn't fit in as a boy.

The Denial of Self

Many HSBs try to deny their true feelings and preferences in an effort to be accepted by other boys. For example, boys frequently insult each other, which can actually become a form of male bonding. Boys may not be accepted by others unless they can take this teasing. This form of male interaction puts the sensitive male, who feels emotional pain deeply, in a tenuous position since he is not able to easily shrug off insults. This is a prime reason why the HSB has a challenging time making and keeping friends.

When HSBs pretend that the insults don't bother them or that they are okay with impersonal, group-based friendships, they are denying their authentic selves. Sensitive boys and men in our society often feel they have to hide their sensitivity, and they do so usually at great personal cost (Aron, 2002).

Dan learned at an early age to deny his real self so that he could fit in with other boys. He never liked football, but after he was humiliated for not knowing about a local NFL football game, he pretended to show an interest in football. "A popular boy in tenth grade, Greg, sat next to me in homeroom. One day he asked me how I liked the big football game that was played over the weekend, and when I responded that I didn't know about any football game, he started laughing at me. He insulted me, saying things like, 'Where do you live, on Mars?' He told the other boys sitting near me that I didn't know about the game, and everyone around me started laughing about how out of it I was. I remember I felt so much shame that I wanted to hide. After that humiliating experience I decided to read the sports page daily, even though I had no interest in football. I just did it to try to be accepted by the other guys, or least not laughed at."

Sometimes sensitive boys develop a form of self-hatred in their attempt to be accepted by the tough male culture. Sadly, many internalize contempt for sensitive males. Ron, a married attorney who was raised in a small town in Connecticut, was shamed for his sensitivity as a young boy and decided to become friends with a group of non-HSBs in middle school. "When I was a shy, fearful boy, I didn't have any friends. But when I pushed myself to act more aggressively, especially around other guys, I was accepted and felt strong compared to when I acted like a wimp. Now I tend to look down on sensitive guys, thinking they're weak."

Ron's strategy may be a common one, as the pressure to conform is extremely strong. However, although Ron eventually felt accepted and befriended, he did so by sacrificing his true feelings and needs. Furthermore, he may have missed out on deep, authentic friendships he could have made with other HSBs. The fact that some HSBs are willing to deny and condemn sensitivity illustrates just how powerful the pressure is to behave like an aggressive male.

Making Friends with Non-HSBs

As we've seen, since the sensitive boy frequently feels intimidated and frightened by aggressive male behavior, it's difficult for him to become friends with the eighty percent of non-HSBs. Gary remembered, "I was so self-conscious as a boy that I tended to spend most of my time alone. Since I wasn't into sports, I always felt different—I wasn't 'one of the guys.' When I saw boys fighting, I would get anxious and want to run away. Whenever I had to hang out with the alpha-male-type guys in the neighborhood, I would get so nervous that I'd be miserable. I couldn't keep up with their countless putdowns or dares and was always in fear of being humiliated."

Even the athletic sensitive boys who played on sports teams never felt like they were one of the boys. Jonathan reported, "I never fit in with the other boys, even though I was good at sports. As soon as the game was over I would want to leave. I'm too sensitive to be around a bunch of guys. When a group of guys gets together they usually interact with each other harshly, which doesn't appeal to me. Whenever I've had to be in a group with a bunch of guys, I've felt like a stranger in a strange land."

Likewise, Joel didn't feel safe being in a group of males. "Ever since I was teased by other boys when I was young I've always felt nervous in a group of men. Most men in a group setting still act like adolescent boys by 'playfully' shaming each other and boasting about their conquests—sexual, economic, or athletic. I prefer to interact with one other sensitive guy who I feel safe with rather than with a group of guys."

The HSB and Sensitive Friends

Several men told me that it's better for the sensitive boy to have just one sensitive friend rather than trying to be accepted by a group of non-HSBs. Ryan told me, "It's important for sensitive boys to make friends with other sensitive guys. They shouldn't spend time hanging out with judgmental non-HSBs who make them feel flawed. The sensitive boy should also resist comparing himself or trying to compete with non-HSBs or he'll start feeling bad about himself. I remember that I hated myself when I was a boy since I couldn't measure up to the tough boys in my neighborhood."

Gary was a very sensitive boy, yet he was one of the few North American HSMs who said he wasn't teased as a child. Gary reported, "I hung out with progressive people in junior and senior high school, so my friends never teased me even though I had bad acne and was emotionally sensitive. I was placed in the advanced academic classes with more mature students, which was probably another reason I wasn't put down. It's important that HSBs surround themselves as much as possible with gentle, compassionate friends. I might not have been so successful in life if I'd been ridiculed for my sensitivity as a boy."

You can help foster your sensitive boy's friendships with other HSBs by actively encouraging these relationships. Instead of trying to push your HSB to befriend neighborhood non-HSBs or to get into group activities that don't interest him, encourage his interest in one-on-one time with friends by inviting friends to the house. Help facilitate your son and his friends to experience activities that interest them and let your son know that you like the friends he's choosing. This support can go along way toward counteracting all the negative messages he's receiving about his friendship preferences.

A Group for HSBs

When a sensitive boy is in a group of like-minded, emotionally sensitive males, he can feel relaxed and safe. Alan said, "I've been in a men's group for sixteen years, which has been probably one of the most healing experiences in my life. It gave me an opportunity to share my emotions and develop positive relationships with men in a safe environment. My closest friends are the men I've come to know and love in the men's group.

"The group has been such a contrast to the shaming experiences I had with other boys while growing up. Even though I had athletic ability and could run really fast, I remember that I couldn't wait to get off the bus after coming home from track meets. It was like a three-ring circus on the bus, with the other boys either putting each other down, snapping towels at each other, or screaming insults at girls we would pass by."

Starting a group for young sensitive boys can help your son to gain this support and camaraderie from an early age. You could start with play groups when your HSB is as young as age two and either stick with this group or help form new ones as your son gets older. Groups like these are an excellent opportunity for your son to make new friends and build his self-esteem. Mother of a three-year-old HSB named Tristan. Rebecca noticed that her son avoids playing with the more aggressive children in his playgroup. He prefers to play by himself or with one other sensitive child. Rebecca has recently begun making play dates for her son with two other sensitive boys, and she is interested in expanding the group. If your son is older, you may want to suggest that it would be helpful for him to connect with new friends who share his temperament and actively help to facilitate a group.

Non-Sensitive Friends and Self-Acceptance

Even though relating to other HSBs may be more comfortable and enriching for your son, learning how to be with non-HSBs can also be of great value as he grows. These interactions may produce some discomfort at first, but as long as the friends involved remain respectful, it could be beneficial for your HSB to learn how to navigate through the majority nonsensitive boy culture. Some HSMs in my survey told me that, even though it was sometimes uncomfortable hanging out with non-HSBs, having had non-HSB friends ultimately helped them to be stronger emotionally.

Hans told me that having non-HSB friends actually increased his self-esteem. "Until my teens I really lived in my own world, going to the library after school by myself, bicycling alone, or going on solitary explorations near my house. When I reached fourteen I realized that I was lonesome and also began getting interested in girls. I thought that girls wouldn't be interested in me if I seemed too weird. I then forced myself to begin getting together with one or two other extroverted classmates after school and on weekends. I felt better about myself through having made and kept those friends, but I also had a hard time keeping up with those guys. I enjoyed feeling like I was finally part of a group, but at the same time I also realized how different I was from my friends. However, hanging out with them toughened me up, which is what I think I needed."

On the other hand, there may be challenges for some sensitive boys who befriend even an accepting non-HSB. Due to the influence of his peers and the media, a sensitive boy may likely negatively compare himself to a non-sensitive, sensation-seeking friend. Terry remembered, "When I was in high school I briefly had a non-HSB friend whom I tried to emulate. Patrick possessed what I thought was the ideal of masculinity. He was a risk-taker, adventurous, athletic, and would never back down from a fight. He had the chutzpah to go up to any girl in school and start a conversation.

"Even though it generally made me feel better about myself that Patrick would hang out with me, I used to end up actually feeling worse about myself since I couldn't keep up with him. He would beat me in everything we competed in, so I ended up feeling like a loser. He just couldn't understand why I would let things bother me and why I wouldn't take risks or stand up for myself, which only reinforced that there was something wrong with me. I remember once when I was at his house, some of his friends came over and started making fun of me. Patrick joined in, probably due to peer pressure, which was the end of the friendship."

Take some time to discuss friendship with your HSB. Emphasize how important it is to be with friends who respect and understand his sensitivity. Support from you can act as a buffer against the fear of losing inappropriate friends. Tom, like Terry, used to compare himself to the tough, outgoing boys in his peer group until his mom intervened. "I always had a feeling that all the other kids were better than me. I would end up comparing myself to the more aggressive boys, like the athletes, and feel terrible about myself. I remember my mom taking me aside and telling me that everyone has different talents and abilities and praising my gentle nature. After that I think I tried to stop comparing myself so much to nonsensitive people. I'm not always successful, but generally I've chosen friends who accept and respect my sensitivity. Perhaps that's because I now value my sensitivity."

Likewise, Bob reported, "When I was younger, I always tried to change myself to fit in. This was really confusing, because I knew that I wasn't really like my friends. Once I began to accept my sensitivity, I stopped pushing myself to be accepted by other guys. I began having better friends with people I had more in common with, both male and female."

Spending Time Alone

Many HSBs enjoy spending solitary time pursuing their interests. Without anyone else around they feel free to concentrate on an activity and feel no pressure to be other than they are. However, there is a tendency for HSBs to spend time alone due to shyness, fear, or feeling like they don't fit in. It's important for your son to create a balance between spending time alone and with friends or he may not learn successful interpersonal skills. If your son is spending most of his time alone, gently encourage him to reach out and make new friends. You can facilitate this project by taking him to classes in things he's interested in, organizing outings for him and a friend, and encouraging him to invite friends over to the house.

However, it's important that you don't make your son feel that there's something wrong with him if he chooses to spend time alone. Steve said, "If my mom had just left me alone instead of telling me that there was something wrong with me for not going out to play with other kids in the neighborhood, I probably would have ventured out in my own time. However, her constant nagging just made me feel worse about myself and made me not want to go out at all." The key is to foster a balance of social and solitary time. Let your HSB know that you support him in spending time alone if he really enjoys it, but also remind him that one or two good friends can really enrich his life. Again, your support and understanding will help empower him to make the decisions that will suit his needs.

Cultural Differences in Friendships

The sensitive men in my study who were raised in India and Thailand were more likely to have more friends than those raised in Denmark or North America. These Asian countries are more communally oriented than the individualistic Western countries, and they tend to respect sensitive males more.

Nui from Thailand stated, "My family and friends noticed my sensitivity, and they always showed me a lot of love and respect for my gentle behavior. In Thailand, people like myself who are kind and caring are always treated with courtesy. I was more sensitive than the other boys in my class, but no one ever teased me for being like that. As a matter of fact, I was elected class president when I was in sixth grade. I always had lots of friends growing up."

It's helpful for parents and HSBs in Western countries to realize that their experiences are, to a large extent, culturally determined. If your HSB were growing up in Thailand, for example, he would likely have more friends and be more readily accepted by his peers. You and your son will be able to feel better about his trait through understanding this global perspective to male sensitivity. Also, like Tun, who was supported by his relatives growing up in Thailand, you can take cues from other cultures in how to raise a more confident and secure child. Implementing a more communally oriented approach to child rearing, as Tun enjoyed, could help your son as he grows.

Siblings of Sensitive Boys

Sibling rivalry between the sensitive boy and his non-sensitive sibling can be extremely disturbing for the HSB. Aaron, who grew up with three older brothers told me, "It was horrendous for me growing up in a family with three aggressive older brothers who used to fight all the time. My parents were so overwhelmed that they didn't bother to stop my brothers from hitting me. They would watch wrestling on TV and then try out all sorts of moves on me. I was terrified of getting hurt, and I remember that they used to pin me down and I would sometimes cry. It was a nightmare at home trying to avoid all the fighting. Everyone in my family thought I was strange because I didn't want to fight. Luckily, I lived on a farm, so I was able to find hiding places away from all the turmoil and danger inside the house. Perhaps putting up with all that abuse from my brothers made me feel unsafe, since I feel like I've been hiding my entire life. I still resent my brothers, and I avoid family get-togethers so I don't have to see them."

Parents can help lessen sibling rivalry by constantly emphasizing the need for each sibling to treat the other with compassion and respect. Parents and extended-family members should explain to the nonsensitive siblings about their sensitive brother's trait of sensitivity and discuss how each child has different positive attributes. Parents need to point out to their nonsensitive children that it is wrong to shame someone for their sensitivity and discuss how negative media stereotypes perpetuate these myths. The following are some suggestions that you could tell your non-HSC:

- Just like everyone likes a different flavor of ice cream, your brother has different interests than you, and that's okay.

- Even though most boys you know may prefer active and loud play, your brother, just like twenty percent of all boys, prefers to play quietly, and his preference needs to be respected.

- I understand that you wish that your brother would play the same games that you like, but let's figure out which activities you both like to do.

- Just like Mom and Dad are quiet when you're sleeping so we don't disturb you, it's important that you respect your brother's need when he asks you to be quiet.

- Although you and your brother are very different, I really appreciate the many wonderful qualities that you each have.

- I know that most of the guys you see on television and in the movies act tough and never show their feelings, but I think it's healthier for men to be kind and sensitive and to express their feelings.

Gary told me that his parents always emphasized that he and his brothers should act kindly toward each other. Gary said, "I had an older brother who was not sensitive, but he always treated me nicely and with respect. He never picked on me or forced me to play the games he liked. My two younger brothers never teased me for being sensitive. I credit my parents for being great role models for us four boys, since they treated each other and all of us in a caring manner. I guess I really lucked out with my parents and brothers."

Birth order can be a factor in the sensitive boy's relationship with his siblings. The oldest child is frequently more self-reliant and usually doesn't compare himself to his younger siblings. He may not be so affected by his younger sibling's opinion of his sensitivity, especially when there is a large age gap between siblings. Lars reported, "I was the oldest of three boys, with my next-younger sibling five years younger than me. I took care of myself and have fond memories of going for nature walks, riding my bike, or reading as a boy. I developed my own interests regardless of what my brothers were into. I never really fought with or compared myself to my younger brothers."

Parents need to be careful to balance the praise they give their children. Several HSMs in my study shared how painful it was when their parents only praised their siblings. If you brag about your popular, extroverted child but do not acknowledge his sensitive brother's positive qualities, it can be devastating to your son's self-esteem. Doug recalled, "I remember being jealous when my parents bragged about how popular my older sister was. I felt like a loser because I didn't have any friends."

If possible, your sensitive son should not be forced to share a room with a non-sensitive sibling, which could be too overstimulating for him. He should have his own room for the quiet and privacy that he needs, but if that's not a possibility make sure that your son's space is quiet and safe (Aron, 2002).

Conclusion

Your HSB's relationships with peers and siblings can be rocky, especially if the kids involved don't understand the positive qualities of the HSB. Helping your HSB find friends who appreciate the benefits of knowing him is a matter of gentle encouragement and support, as well as some hands-on planning and hosting. As always, your support will be invaluable to your son, not only in helping him expand his social world, but also by letting him know that you are always there to support him.

Additionally, it's the adults' job in a family to help regulate the behavior of siblings. Do not put up with sibling teasing based on your HSB's sensitive traits. Sure, siblings fight, and sometimes they're not so kind to each other. However, picking on an HSB for being sensitive can be particularly hurtful and should not be tolerated. Encourage your kids to notice each other's positive qualities and let them know that you expect them to show each other kindness and respect.

Next we'll examine the role of athletics in the lives of HSBs.

Chapter 6

Boys and Sports: Playing Under Pressure

"I dreaded going to gym class when I was in school since I was always afraid of being laughed at and humiliated whenever I dropped a baseball or football. P.E. class destroyed my self-worth and confidence more than anything when I was a boy."

"I guess I was an average athlete, but my dad would spend hours with me, showing me how to play soccer, baseball, and basketball since he loved those sports. In retrospect, I'm glad Dad helped me since I felt better about myself being able to play well on team sports."

Sports can play a large role in the lives of children, and traditionally, being good at sports is an important factor in masculinity. Your HSB may be interested in sports and want to participate—or he may not. His relationship to sports can have a strong impact on his self-image and feelings of self-worth, so we'll be taking a close look at this relationship in this chapter. We'll consider the importance that sports play in most boys' lives and how athletic activities affect the sensitive boy, and then we will investigate which form of physical exercise is best for your son and the need for the sensitive boy to learn self-defense.

Sensitive Boys and Sports

When a boy becomes involved in sports, he feels accepted by his peers, which increases his self-esteem. Boys frequently compete in sports to prove that they are "man enough" (Pittman, 1994). Most boys are involved in some team sports (Gurian, 1996), which is in stark contrast to the experiences of most HSBs. My research indicated that eighty-five percent of sensitive boys did not participate in team sports and most of the HSMs reported that throughout their life they preferred to participate in individual exercise. Since HSBs do not perform well under group pressure and may be deeply hurt by the cruel culture of malicious "boy teasing" while playing sports with other boys, they generally avoid such interactions.

The competitive sports culture is anathema for many sensitive boys, yet boys who aren't athletic tend to feel undervalued and suffer socially (Kindlon and Thompson, 1999). Nonathletic boys may be ostracized or teased if they aren't adept in team sports, which is particularly painful for the sensitive boy. However, some HSMs said that they were naturally athletic and were able to cope with the pressure of team sports as a boy. Regardless of athletic ability, it's important for the sensitive boy to participate in physical exercise since it will help him become healthier and stronger, reduce stress and increase joy through endorphin release, and help him to release negative energy that he has absorbed during the day.

Challenges of HSBs Playing Sports in School

Steve's memories about having to attend physical education class in school epitomize some of the difficulties that the sensitive boy faces regarding team sports. Steve remembered, "I felt overwhelmed by group pressure when I was forced to play sports in school. In gym class, I was always one of the last boys chosen to play on a team. The aggressive team captains complained that there was no one left to pick as a few of us shy, nonathletic boys stood around feeling humiliated. I remember once it was my turn at bat during a softball game and a good athlete in my class, Paul, told me he wanted to bat for me since I'd just get an out and lose the game for our team.

"To avoid further shame, I avoided all physical activity as a boy. However, as an adult I found out that I actually enjoyed some sports. A friend of mine, Bob, showed me how to play baseball when I was in my early twenties and encouraged me to join a team he was playing on. I never let the other players know how much anxiety and fear I experienced when they were watching me trying to catch a ball being thrown to me at first base or when I was up to bat. However, I did persevere and enjoyed the camaraderie and acceptance of playing on a team with other guys. I only wish that someone had showed me how to play baseball as a boy."

Steve's childhood experiences illustrates how emotionally damaging it can be for the sensitive boy to be shamed in the cruel, competitive boy culture. However, like the adult Steve, if a sensitive male had someone to teach and encourage him how to play, he could thrive, even in the insensitive world of male sports. Later in the chapter, I'll introduce many methods to help increase your son's self-esteem by showing him how to cope with team sports.

Looking for Acceptance Through Sports

Some sensitive boys deny who they are in order to be accepted by their athletic non-HSB peers. Gary recounted, "When I was in high school, I played the flute in the school band. It was bad enough being in the band, but playing the flute always made me feel like I was effeminate. It was kind of bizarre the way there seemed to be a hierarchy of 'masculine' activities in high school. Playing football or any sport was considered much more masculine than playing in the band, and playing instruments like the trumpet or drums was considered more masculine than playing the flute.

"I felt so much inner torment that I actually quit band, which I loved, and went out for football and track, which I didn't enjoy as much. I mean, I wasn't having as much fun, but at least I could think of myself as more manly. How sad that I felt the need to give up something I loved merely to ease an inner torment I felt as a result of prejudice against sensitive males."

Doug also felt he had to engage in a pretense in order to be accepted by his peers: "When I was growing up, if you didn't want to play rough-and-tumble sports you ran the risk of being called a sissy. Although sensitive guys are not big on participating in contact sports such as football, when I was in high school I went out for the team. I hated it, but I played on the team because that's what my friends did. Why didn't I quit? It was an ego thing, meant to prove that even though I was sensitive, I was a still a real man. I felt as though I would lose my friends if I didn't try to fit in and be a 'real' guy."

Ryan, now a graduate student at UCLA, also denied his sensitivity until he became an adult. He told me, "When I was in grade school I used to get teased for being shy, and I never played with the other boys. As I got older I desperately wanted to fit in, so in middle school I started playing basketball and soccer. I also took up surfing, which is really popular here in Southern California. I suppose that I got involved in these sports that I really didn't enjoy that much in order to prove that I wasn't a wuss.

"The summer after I graduated high school I used to play b-ball several times a week with some tough-acting dudes at a basketball court near my house. Now I wonder what motivated me to play under such intense conditions, and I can only conclude that my desire to prove that I was a real man was greater than my respect for my sensitive nature. I can honestly say that I rarely enjoyed myself playing ball with those tough guys since I had to be on guard against humiliation if I made a mistake.

"However, when I began graduate school last year I started seeing a therapist and am beginning to learn to accept myself. My therapist told me that I have a finely tuned nervous system, and now I take better care of myself. I've recently stopped my involvement in competitive and dangerous sports and now pursue activities that I thoroughly enjoy like hiking and bicycling. What a relief not to have to try to prove myself anymore."

Gary, Doug, and Ryan believed the societal myth that to be a "real man" you have to act in a rough, aggressive manner and prove your manhood through intense athletic competition. When sensitive males deny their authentic, gentle nature to validate a false sense of masculinity, they frequently give up what they enjoy, which can cause emotional torment and a sense of anomie. Throughout the book we will discuss how your son can let go of society's false beliefs of masculinity so that he can appreciate his true nature.

Athletic HSBs

As you may recall, some of the sensitive men in my survey enjoyed playing team sports during their childhood. In my study I found that the more athletically inclined men had higher self-esteem than those HSMs who did not participate in team sports as a boy. Christoffer from Denmark said, "I have always loved playing around with all kinds of balls, especially a soccer ball. Being a good soccer player has made me feel good about myself since I was accepted by the other guys on my team and the girls in my school admired me. Not only did playing soccer make me feel that I was normal, but I found playing soccer gave me a sense of freedom and happiness."

Similarly, Peter, the musician from San Diego, shared how his involvement in sports helped him. "I loved playing football when I was a boy, especially running and catching the ball. I was bigger than most boys and good at football, so even though my dad humiliated me for my sensitivity—even calling me a faggot sometimes—I was accepted by my peers. I think I would have been a real mess if I wasn't athletic."

Jonathan, the financial planner from Philadelphia, also had many positive experiences playing team sports. "I loved to play sports when I was a boy and enjoyed being on my Little League baseball team. I ran cross-country and participated in long-distance events in track and field in high school. I enjoyed the way running cleared my head, and I liked the challenge of pushing myself. However, I didn't like the competitiveness that the coaches emphasized, and when the event was over I didn't want to hang out with the other guys.

"I took up ice hockey in college because I had loved watching hockey as I was growing up. Another reason may have been to prove I was tough." Since hockey can be a violent sport, I was surprised that a highly sensitive male like Jonathan was an avid hockey player and fan. In our interview, Jonathan told me that he avoided violence and fighting as a boy, and he described himself as someone who is gentle and a peacemaker.

Jonathan explained this apparent contradiction: "While professional hockey is rampant with fighting, this never happened on the teams I played on at the college level. I would find it difficult sometimes when there was contact with other players, but I was so focused on my playing that I didn't worry about the contact. When I watch professional hockey, I frequently cringe and feel disgusted by the fighting. However, I do respect the finesse of players like Gretzky and Lemieux. I used to like going to watch professional hockey, but now I won't go to the games since it's such an assault on my senses. I much rather watch the game on TV in peace and quiet at home."

So, as in any group, some HSBs have a natural athletic ability and some do not. Also, along the continuum of sensitivity, some HSBs can tolerate the stimulation of team sports while others dislike this aspect. The key is to find athletic activities that your HSB authentically enjoys—supporting him if he prefers to eschew team sports and helping him to get involved in physical activities that work for him.

Which Physical Activity Is Best for My HSB?

After reading these stories about sensitive boys and sports you are probably wondering which sport is best for your son. Will your son's self-esteem be hurt, like Steve's was, if he is humiliated by being forced to play team sports in school? Or, like Gary, should he be exposed to competitive sports to help him learn how to get along with the eighty percent non-HSBs? Even if your HSB is not enthusiastic about team sports, as long as he feels safe and is interested in a sport, it would be good for him to be involved in a group physical activity. With your support, this involvement can help him learn to navigate through the aggressive, competitive world of boys. Just remember that his experience should be positive and increase his self-esteem.

Before your son joins a team, you should talk with the coach and possibly other parents to make sure that the players are treated with respect and are not overly competitive. If your son wants to play on a team, I recommend that he choose a sport that is inherently less violent, such as soccer or volleyball, rather than American football or rugby. However, any player or coach with an insensitive attitude to win at all costs could turn any game into a nightmare for a sensitive boy. Unfortunately, we are still living in a culture where "winning isn't everything, it's the only thing." Actually, any sport can be enjoyable if the consciousness of the participants is supportive and caring (Zeff, 2004).

I know a fourteen-year-old HSB from Santa Barbara, California named Cody who took up tennis at his father's urging. When Cody played tennis with a supportive friend he excelled in the sport. However, whenever he played with very competitive players, he told me that he would feel overwhelmed by the pressure of having to perform and would usually end up losing those matches. Your HSB may very well have a similar experience, so it's important to help him feel supported and relaxed when he competes in any sport. If he doesn't, it may be time to find another sport to try.

However, if your son is not interested in team sports, I would suggest that he take up an individual sport such as swimming, bicycling, or working out at the gym. Even shy, nonathletic HSBs will shine when they are involved in an athletic activity that they enjoy. Once your son realizes that he is adept in one area, it will give him more confidence to participate in other physical activities. It's money well spent to provide lessons for your son to learn tennis, basketball, soccer, or martial arts so that he can feel good about himself. And, as always, your loving support is the key to making this exploration fun and safe rather than leaving your HSB feeling as though he is failing.

A Paradox: The Sensitive Male Hunter

While over ninety percent of sensitive males in my research abhorred violence and stated that they were concerned with the humane treatment of animals, surprisingly, several HSMs mentioned that they enjoyed hunting throughout their life. The HSMs who hunted had been raised in rural areas where the sport was popular. Aaron, who was raised on a farm, told me, "I loved hunting with a BB gun and a small-bore rifle when I was a boy. As an adult, I've always enjoyed hunting when I can go to the bush for a few weeks each year and never see another person." Hunting provided an opportunity for Aaron to be alone in nature. While most sensitive males would choose hiking or camping in nature rather than hunting, Aaron's experience illustrates that each sensitive male has different proclivities. As a group, HSBs are not monolithic, so it's important to be open to your son's preferences instead of assuming he will or won't enjoy a specific activity.

Self-Defense and the HSB

Most sensitive boys probably won't be attracted to most martial arts, boxing, or wrestling. These sports can place too much emphasis on violence and be too stimulating for the HSB. However, learning some form of self-defense can really empower a sensitive boy, helping him feel safe and able to fend off bullies. You might help your HSB feel more comfortable in this endeavor by inviting one of his friends to join him when he takes self-defense lessons, or you could have your son take individual self-defense lessons if it's too intimidating for him to be in a group setting. It's important to let the instructor know that your son is sensitive and needs support from the trainer.

Tom, who had been taunted by other children in both grade school and middle school, remembered, "When I was in high school I finally got sick and tired of being pushed around by several bullies and began learning karate. Since I don't like fighting, I felt scared and anxious when I first started the lessons, and I found it especially difficult to spar with the other students. However, after several months of practicing karate, I remember feeling more confident and less fearful, and I don't remember anyone pushing me around after that. I only wish that I had learned how to defend myself when I was younger."

Judy, a divorced mother of a twelve-year-old HSB, was very upset when he came home from school one day bruised and crying. Tyler had always been a fearful, shy and emotionally sensitive boy, just the type that the bullies like to attack. Tyler told his mom that a big boy in the eighth grade jumped him after school when he got on his bike to ride home. Evidently the boy had been bullying him since he started seventh grade a few months earlier.

Angry and distressed, Judy told Tyler that she was going to call the principal, but Tyler was afraid that that would just make things worse. After discussing the situation with Tyler's dad, who lived in another state, Judy decided to sign him up for classes in aikido. While Tyler was frightened when he first started the self-defense class, he soon became comfortable as he got to know the friendly and supportive teacher and other students. After four months of studying aikido, Judy noticed that her son appeared happier and more confident. She mentioned that her son was able to set boundaries for the first time in his life. The sensitive boy who masters some form of self-defense becomes less fearful, more confident and frequently more sociable.

Cultural Differences in Attitudes Toward Sports

Again, it's useful to look at how attitudes about sports differ from country to country. It will increase your son's self-worth knowing that sensitive boys in other countries are not shamed when they participate in team sports.

Sensitive boys growing up in Denmark, Thailand, and India had different experiences about participation in team sports than those from North America. And, though team-sport participation may be just as popular in Europe as in the United States, it appears that Danish sensitive boys are not humiliated for a lack of athletic ability.

However, even some of these Danish HSMs felt different as boys because they didn't want to participate in team sports. Jorgen, a divorced salesman from Copenhagen, said, "I always felt like the odd man out when boys in school would play group sports. Although no one ever gave me a bad time for not participating, I noticed that the most popular guys played on our school soccer team. Throughout my life, my main physical activity has been bicycling, which I really enjoy. I'm presently training for a 300-kilometer tour with a friend, and I've felt really good about myself since I took up long-distance cycling."

Tun, who was raised in Thailand, noted, "Other students acknowledged you if you were a good athlete in school, but no one really cared that much if you played sports or not. There was one guy in my class who practiced Thai boxing and martial arts, but I think he would have been just as well liked if he didn't master those sports. Being good at sports was just not that important among the students in my school in Thailand."

Raised in India, Ashok said, "I don't recall anyone ever being teased for not being athletic. In school, all of the kids played group sports together. Everyone was included and the boys were always considerate. No one ever teased or laughed at the less-talented boys when we played cricket, volleyball, or soccer.

"I wasn't really that interested in sports, but some of my friends asked me to join the badminton team when I was in high school. I ended up being the captain of the team and had to practice a lot for tournaments in my district and state. Although the other boys seemed to care more about winning than me, I don't remember anyone ever pressuring me to be more competitive."

Love and Empathy in Sports

I am concluding this chapter about sensitive boys and sports with a story that illustrates the potential for boys to treat others with love and empathy while playing team sports. The self-help author and lecturer Wayne Dyer shared the following story about a father and his mentally and physically handicapped boy on a PBS television show called *The Power of Intention.*

"My son and I were walking past a park where some boys were playing baseball. Shay asked, 'Do you think they'll let me play?' I knew that most of the boys would not want someone like Shay on their team; but as a father, I also understood that if my son were allowed to play, it would give him a much-needed sense of belonging and some confidence to be accepted by others in spite of his handicaps.

"I approached one of the boys on the field and asked (not expecting much) if Shay could play. The boy looked around for guidance and said, 'We're losing by six runs and the game is in the eighth inning. I guess he can be on our team, and we'll try to put him in to bat in the ninth inning.'

"Shay struggled over to the team's bench and, with a broad smile, put on a team shirt. I watched with a small tear in my eye and warmth in my heart. The boys saw my joy at my son being accepted. In the bottom of the eighth inning, Shay's team scored a few runs but was still behind by three. In the top of the ninth inning, Shay put on a glove and played in the right field. Even though no hits came his way, he was obviously ecstatic just to be in the game and on the field, grinning from ear to ear as I waved to him from the stands.

"In the bottom of the ninth inning, Shay's team scored again. Now, with two outs and the bases loaded, the potential winning run was on base and Shay was scheduled to be next at bat. At this juncture, did they let Shay bat and give away their chance to win the game?

Surprisingly, Shay was given the bat. Everyone knew that a hit was all but impossible because Shay didn't even know how to hold the bat properly, much less connect with the ball. However, as Shay stepped up to the plate, the pitcher, recognizing that the other team was putting winning aside for this moment in Shay's life, moved in a few steps to lob the ball in softly so Shay could at least make contact.

"The first pitch came and Shay swung clumsily and missed. The pitcher again took a few steps forward to toss the ball softly towards Shay. As the pitch came in, Shay swung at the ball and hit a slow ground ball right back to the pitcher. The game would now be over.

The pitcher picked up the soft grounder and could have easily thrown the ball to the first baseman. Shay would have been out, and that would have been the end of the game. Instead, the pitcher threw the ball right over the first baseman's head, out of reach of all teammates.

"Everyone from the stands and both teams started yelling, 'Shay, run to first! Run to first!' Never in his life had Shay ever run that far, but he made it to first base. He scampered down the baseline, wide-eyed and startled. Everyone yelled, 'Run to second, run to second!' Catching his breath, Shay awkwardly ran towards second, gleaming and struggling to make it to the base. By the time Shay rounded towards second base, the right fielder had the ball, the smallest guy on their team, who now had his first chance to be the hero for his team.

"He could have thrown the ball to the second baseman for the tag, but he understood the pitcher's intentions, so he, too, intentionally threw the ball high and far over the third baseman's head. Shay ran toward third base deliriously as the runners ahead of him circled the bases toward home. All were screaming, 'Shay, Shay, Shay, all the way, Shay!' Shay reached third base because the opposing shortstop ran to help him by turning him in the direction of third base, and shouted, 'Run to third! Shay, run to third!' As Shay rounded third, the boys from both teams and the spectators were on their feet, screaming, 'Shay, run home! Run home!' Shay ran to home, stepped on the plate, and was cheered as the hero who hit the grand slam and won the game for his team.

"'That day,' said the father softly, with tears now rolling down his face, 'the boys from both teams helped bring a piece of true love and humanity into this world.' Shay didn't make it to another summer. He died that winter, having never forgotten being the hero and making me so happy, as well as coming home and experiencing his mother tearfully embracing her little hero of the day!'"

This touching story illustrates that all boys have the potential to treat the gentle, nonathletic, and sensitive boy with respect. It is my hope that all boys will learn to play sports in a compassionate, inclusive, and brotherly manner so that no one is humiliated or shamed. Through caring coaches and players, we can all be part of a global movement to bring humanity back into the world of male sports like the empathetic boys who encouraged Shay to feel good about himself.

Conclusion

A relationship with athletics can be either a challenge or great joy for the HSB (and sometimes both!). While team sports in schools can often become a bastion of insensitive and sometimes cruel boy behavior, sports can also boost your HSB's self-esteem and help him find camaraderie with other boys.

The highly sensitive boy needs support to be able to decide whether or not he wishes to pursue team sports or do another form of physical activity that's more solitary. As long as this decision isn't based on fear—his fear of being humiliated and rejected or your fears about ensuring the "normalcy" of your boy—your HSB will feel free to make the choice that feels right for him. And, if the sport he chooses turns out to be a bad fit for him, help him find another physical activity that is more suited to his temperament. As long as his choices and needs are honored, the HSB will be able to pursue the physical activity that best suits him.

As we've seen, sports and physical activity can be a boon to the HSB's self-esteem. Next we'll move on to some other options available for helping your HSB realize his own self-worth.

Chapter 7

Raising the Sensitive Boy's Self-Esteem

"There was one guy I envied in middle school, Scott. All the girls liked him because he was tall, buffed, and good-looking, and I hated my body since I was the opposite: short, skinny, and plagued with acne. I've worried about my bodily imperfections my entire life."

"I guess I've always been spiritual. Even in elementary school I was interested in books about great saints, and then I started meditating in high school. I never bought into the superficial, materialistic American lifestyle, and I always appreciated my sensitivity since it helped me have profound spiritual experiences."

In the preceding chapter, we examined how physical activity can help a boy's self-esteem. This is partly due to the feeling of strength and self-efficacy that sports can foster. After all, when your body works well, you generally feel better about yourself. Thus, in this chapter we'll take a closer look at how body image and general health affects the self-esteem of boys, and I'll offer some powerful methods to improve your son's relationship with his physical self.

However, it's clear that self-esteem isn't just about the body. Many find great strength and comfort in a feeling of connection with a spiritual power. Finding meaning in everyday life can infuse an HSB with a sense of purpose, and he will likely get a subsequent boost in his self-worth. So, I will end this chapter with a discussion about spirituality and the HSB.

Body Image and Boys

Emphasis on male body image has significantly increased in the last thirty-five years due to influence by the media. Male eating disorders were almost unknown in the 1970s, yet today they are increasing at a significant rate (Pope, Phillips, and Olivardia). Recent studies show that the connection between a poor body image and low self-esteem is actually higher among men than women (2002).

Research has shown that a majority of boys choose a body ideal that most men can attain only with steroids (Pope, Phillips, and Olivardia, 2002). In one study by researcher Dan Moore, one-third of the normal-weight boys were dissatisfied with their weight, with two thirds of those boys believing that they were underweight. Another study found that boys are even more dissatisfied with their bodies than girls are. As early as 1993, the *New England Journal of Medicine* published an article showing that six percent of all high-school boys have taken steroids in order to become more muscular, and the usage has been increasing since then (Pope, Phillips, and Olivardia, 2002).

Most boys' self-esteem suffers due to a false image of what a boy or man is supposed to look like. It's difficult for males to feel good about themselves when they try to measure up to the elusive image of the abnormally muscular media superhero. As has happened with girls, boys' images of their bodies can become highly skewed, resulting in a drastically flawed perception of how they look to others. *Body dysmorphic disorder* is a psychological disorder in which the afflicted person is excessively concerned with and preoccupied by a perceived defect in his physical features, when in fact he or she looks fine to others. Recently, body dysmorphic disorder has been refined to include an almost exclusively male variety: *muscle dysmorphia*. This variant includes an intense focus on muscularity and the resultant shame and embarrassment when the male inevitably realizes he doesn't match up to his skewed expectations. These painful feelings arise in the face of the cultural notion that muscular bodies symbolize power, virility, and masculinity (Pope, Phillips, and Olivardia, 2002).

Many studies have shown that the more dissatisfied a boy is with his body, the poorer his self-esteem. In fact, body image has been shown to be the greatest single predictor of self-esteem (Pope, Phillips, and Olivardia, 2002). A boy who is teased by his peers about his body is at risk of developing body or muscle dysmorphic disorder and the sensitive boy is particularly vulnerable to this disorder since, as previously mentioned, he reacts more deeply to teasing than non-HSBs.

The Media's Influence on HSBs' Body Image

Throughout their life, males have been bombarded with advertisements showing lean and muscular bodies, implying that if you don't look like the ad you should worry. If men didn't buy into these images, advertisers would never sell their products and the industry would not make billions of dollars annually on all sorts of products that are supposed to improve the appearance of the male body (Pope, Phillips, and Olivardia, 2002).

The average American child attends school for 900 hours a year but watches 1500 hours of TV a year (Gurian, 1996). The media is saturated with ads of blemish-free, strikingly handsome men with no body fat, six-pack abs of steel, and huge biceps and pecs. In addition, boys are frequently exposed to violence in the media, such as brutal ultimate fighting and vicious wrestling bouts starring grotesque and disproportionately huge men. It is estimated that internationally half a billion males weekly watch violent, steroid-induced wrestlers smash each other (Pope, Phillips, and Olivardia, 2002).

Most of the male movie stars before 1970 had ordinary physiques that didn't require steroid use or going to the gym every day. However, the image of the male in the movies nowadays gives the wrong message of what it means to be a man. In the 1970s, media idols included Clint Eastwood and Charles Bronson and the macho, violent characters they played. In the '80s and '90s, Sylvester Stallone and Arnold Schwarzenegger were the steroid-pumped raging "heroes" the media emphasized. And now we have even more outsized actors featured—men like Vin Diesel or Dwayne Johnson ("The Rock"), who originally came from the super-violent pro-wrestling circuit. These unrealistically macho superheroes are the current models for young males to learn what it means to be a man.

However, as our societal view of masculinity is slowly beginning to change, I have a glimmer of hope that gentleness in males will gradually become more accepted in the media and that the movie industry and television will show more sensitive, normal-looking men in a positive light. The media eventually responds to consumers' wishes and pressure, so men can object to these stereotypical and deforming portrayals just as other under- and negatively represented groups have. It's imperative that parents and sensitive men let the industry know that they want to see more sensitive, average-looking males in the media.

Additionally, as someone of influence in your HSB's life, you have the power to defuse some of these potentially damaging images. Be vigilant about the media your HSB consumes. For younger kids, you can restrict violent, pumped-up male images from your TV and computer screens. For an older HSB who has more access to media, you can discuss these images with him, helping him put these fantasy physiques into perspective. Helping your HSB use his critical-thinking skills and supporting him in being just who he is can go a long way toward mitigating these persistent media messages.

Body Image and Self-Esteem in the HSB

According to my survey of HSMs, the sensitive boy tends to be more vulnerable to developing body or muscle dysmorphic disorder than other boys. As I mentioned in Chapter Four, sensitive boys are reluctant to defend themselves or retaliate against bullying and become more upset than other boys when they are teased. So when your HSB experiences the unfortunately typical boy teasing about some perceived defect in his physicality, he will tend to take it harder than other boys. Unfortunately, as a sensitive boy becomes more upset, the taunting generally increases. Since sensitive children have a tendency to be self-critical, he is more likely to believe the put-downs and look for imperfections in his body.

Some North American HSBs reported being teased about their body features and agonizing over their physical appearance. Terry, who was teased for being skinny, became fixated with getting bigger as an adult. "Although I was skinny and probably weaker than other boys, I felt that my overreaction to being teased was probably what made the boys in school humiliate me all the time. In seventh grade they used to call me a weakling, and I remember trying to hold back tears while I was being taunted. I remember that some other boys in my class were also skinny, but if anyone tried to tease them they would fight back either verbally or physically, which put an end to the put-downs.

"However, when I was twenty-two I bought a weight set and began working out. Pumping iron did work. I went from 130 pounds to 160 pounds in a year and finally looked buffed. I guess I sort of became obsessed with getting bigger since I have religiously continued to work out daily and take lots of muscle-building supplements, probably because I'm afraid that I will be laughed at if I look weak again."

Gary remembered, "I have always been tall and thin. Growing up, it seemed to me that all the men who were portrayed positively in the popular media appeared to be athletic, with well-muscled and toned bodies. As a kid, I can remember the ads in the magazines for protein powder to help you build a muscle-bound body that all the girls were sure to love. Since I was built like the proverbial kid who got sand kicked in his face at the beach by the bigger, more muscular boys, I had a certain envy of those built more to the societal standard. I hated my body.

"I was unaware at the time that most males with my build could never achieve the overly muscled bodies of magazine advertisements without steroids, no matter how much protein powder they consumed or weights they lifted. It wasn't until I went to medical school that I learned that ectomorphs, like myself, just don't have the physical structure to become well-muscled mesomorphs. The irony is that I am quite athletic and have a natural grace and comfort in my body, but I never really appreciated it because I always wanted to look like the buffed guys in the media."

Doug began obsessing about imperfections in his body when he was a teenager. He said, "I could see the veins on my chest when I looked in the mirror and thought that was awful. No one else ever even commented on it, but I was bothered by it for many years. Sometimes I would obsess on this one bodily imperfection for hours. As an adult I gained weight, so my veins no longer showed, but now I'm really worried about losing my hair. I've tried hair-growing formulas and hair transplants on my scalp. I want to keep my hair forever and have spent a lot of time and money trying to avoid losing my hair."

Like their thinner counterparts, overweight sensitive boys are also at risk of developing body dysmorphic disorder and low self-esteem. Joel said, "I used to be teased in school for being overweight, which I'm sure has affected my self-esteem my entire life. I remember being embarrassed whenever I went swimming at summer camp because I didn't want anyone to see my fat body. However, as an adult I started running and cycling, and my body has been at a normal weight since then. However, I still have an image of myself as a fat, ugly boy."

Sensitive Boys with Bigger Frames

Males are usually impressed by big men. The bigger boys in school usually get respect, while smaller boys are made to feel less manly. This can cause the boy with a smaller frame to overachieve in order to gain respect (Kindlon and Thompson, 1999). Since height is frequently associated with masculine power and strength, tall boys are usually favored in all aspects of society. Studies have shown that tall men earn more money and virtually all of the superheroes in the media are tall men. Therefore many men are dissatisfied with their height (Pope, Phillips, and Olivardia, 2002).

Yet, as I noted previously, physical characteristics such as weight, height, or wearing glasses are not necessarily correlated with being bullied. Sometimes boys with larger frames are singled out, too. One very tall HSM, Tom, reported, "I was an easy target because I was tall for my age. This made me very self-conscious, and I was teased constantly about my height. Since I didn't want to fight, it probably made some of those boys feel strong to tease a tall, sensitive boy who wouldn't fight back."

Tom's story may indicate that being targeted for abuse is less about actual physical traits than about attitude. His self-consciousness about his height and his unwillingness to defend himself may have had more to do with his experience of being teased than his actual body type. It seems that the HSBs who exhibited confidence about their bodies (even if they didn't necessarily always feel it) were less vulnerable to teasing and abuse.

For instance, none of the North American sensitive males in my study who regularly participated in team sports, regardless of their physique, were teased. Perhaps this is because they had the confidence of knowing that they were part of a team and that their bodies could function well, having been put to the test. Alan told me, "Although I was considered skinny growing up, it never bothered me. All my friends were skinny, but since we were runners, we were admired for our athletic ability. As a matter of fact, I always had a good body image since I was athletic growing up, playing on a Little League baseball team and on the school basketball team."

So, the key to helping your HSB with his body image (and, subsequently, his self-esteem) may be to support him in being proud of who he is and how he's built. Finding an athletic outlet that he enjoys and that helps him to gain a sense of his own physical abilities can boost his confidence and give him the self-assurance to walk tall, regardless of his body type.

Improving Your HSB's Body Image

Though the media can be a strong influence on your HSB, as an adult in his life you are the stronger influence. Take the opportunity to discuss how the media is perpetuating myths about what a male body should look like and the detrimental effects that unrealistic, macho superheroes have on boys. Teach him that masculinity is not measured by appearance and that muscularity is not masculinity (Pope, Phillips, and Olivardia, 2002). Male adults in particular need to let the HSB know that his body is perfect exactly as it is. Parents, extended family members, coaches, and other adults in the community need to enlighten boys about the dangers of emulating the media-created, steroid-induced, abnormally huge men.

Keep an eye out for a preoccupation with appearance in your HSB. Does he seem to spend an inordinate amount of time focusing on one part of his body, an emphasis that interferes with his school or social life? If you discuss a bodily fixation that your HSB has, he may deny a preoccupation with his body since society shames males into believing that if they are concerned about their appearance they are too feminine.

If you suspect that your HSB has a fixation about a body feature, just listen to him and let him talk about his fear about his perceived imperfection. Reassure him that he looks fine exactly as he is. Encourage him to pursue other interests such as hobbies, friends, or academic skills so that he will focus on his positive attributes. Don't ever criticize or tease your son about his appearance. However, if your son develops a full-blown case of body or muscle dysmorphic disorder, cognitive behavioral therapy could be helpful. For more information about this disorder, visit www.bddcentral.com.

Your HSB's Health

An important aspect of body image and a feeling of general well-being involves general health. It's hard to feel good about yourself or your body if you're frequently ill and feel as though your body doesn't work well. So, keeping your son healthy is important to both how he feels in his body and how he feels about himself.

According to Kenneth Pelletier, an internationally known specialist in stress reduction, between fifty to eighty percent of all diseases have stress-related origins (1977). Since the sensitive boy may be more vulnerable to stress and feeling overwhelmed than the non-HSB, it's important to help him maintain a preventative health-maintenance program, even if he has a strong immune system. The HSB tends to experience illness and pain more deeply than others and may become more upset when he gets sick.

While many HSMs reported having a strong immune system, a large minority of sensitive males in my survey said that they have a weak immune system. Although the small study is not statistically significant, I found it interesting that thirty percent of the HSMs stated that they experienced fewer flus and colds than most people; forty-five percent said they get more flus and colds than others; and twenty-five percent stated the number of flus and colds they got were the same as others. Some of the HSMs who stated they had a weak immune system felt bad about themselves for being sickly. Terry told me, "Probably due to all the stress I encountered as a boy at home and at school, I used to get sick a lot as a child. One time I was lying in bed, sick with a flu, and I remember comparing myself to the strong, athletic boys in my school who never seemed to get sick. My frequent illnesses made me feel like I was weak." So, as Terry lay there feeling physically rotten, his emotions were also stirred up because of his perceived physical defects.

Improving Your HSB's Health

If your HSB tends to have a weak immune system, make sure he eats a healthy diet by increasing his intake of organic fruits and vegetables, complete protein, and whole grains while abstaining from foods like sugar, processed foods, and foods produced with pesticides. In addition, you could discuss with your pediatrician or health care practitioner which supplements could increase your son's energy and boost his immune system. It's crucial that your son exercises daily to maintain optimal health (with his doctor's consent).

Your Son's Doctor

Let your HSB's doctor know about your boy's trait of high sensitivity. Tell the doctor that since your son feels things more deeply, his body could react to medication and pain more intensely than other children. This is important information for the physician to know. If your HSB is afraid of medical treatment, alert the medical staff so that they can help alleviate his fear.

Joel recalled, "When I was a boy, I was terrified whenever I had to get shots at my doctor's office. I was totally embarrassed whenever my mom would tell me that big boys shouldn't get upset from an injection, and my doctor's stern manner sure didn't help me feel comfortable." If your HSB's doctor seems impatient with or unconcerned about his temperament, you should find a new physician. Even though most allopathic doctors (physicians practicing traditional western medicine) are not highly sensitive, there are many physicians with a compassionate bedside manner. Don't settle for less.

A supportive parent is a godsend for the sensitive boy with fears about medical treatment, especially since society expects boys to act tough and never show that they are afraid. Jerry remembered, "My mom was very supportive of me whenever I had to see our family physician, Dr. Kantor, as a boy. I fainted once when I had a blood test and developed a phobia of getting blood drawn. When I was twelve I remember my mom telling me that passing out was nothing to be ashamed of. She made me feel better when she mentioned that a big football player on our local high school team had once fainted when he went for a blood test at Dr. Kantor's office."

Utilizing holistic health practitioners may be a good approach for improving your son's health, since they treat the entire person rather than just symptoms and many of them are HSPs. You may want to consider some of the following alternative healing modalities for you son: aromatherapy, ayurveda, chiropractic, flower remedies, herbal medicine, holistic medical doctors, homeopathy, and naturopathy. In my book *The Highly Sensitive Person's Survival Guide*, I offer extensive information about these alternative healing modalities and ways you can find a qualified practitioner (2004). Make sure that you check with your physician before employing an alternative health practitioner's suggestions.

Sleeping Well

To help your HSB function optimally throughout the day he needs a sufficient amount of sleep. He must be well rested to face the rigors of daily stimulation. Many sensitive boys need more sleep than nonsensitive children, and some HSBs may have trouble falling or staying asleep due to their sensitive nervous system. The following bedtime suggestions will help your son get a good night's sleep:

- Your son's room should be quiet, dark, and at a cool temperature. You may want to have a nightlight and a fan or white-noise machine in his room. The bedroom should be a safe and nurturing space.

- An hour before going to sleep, make sure that your HSB turns off all stimulating electronic equipment. It could be helpful if you either read your young HSB a pleasant story or gently massage him. Older HSBs may want to listen to a relaxation CD or read an uplifting book like *Chicken Soup for the Teenage Soul* before going to sleep (1997).

- Since your son may easily absorb frightening, violent images from the media, which will negatively affect his sleep, carefully monitor his use of media.

- He should go to bed early and not look at the clock after 8 P.M.

- He could either write down or discuss with you solutions to any problems at bedtime, followed by a review of all the positive aspects of his life.

- It's beneficial to go to bed and get up at the same time each day, although this may be challenging for the teenage HSB.

- You could put an aromatherapy diffuser in his room with essential oil of lavender, which is said to induce relaxation. And/or, before bedtime he could take a warm bath with essential oil of lavender or Epsom salts.

For more information about treating sleep problems visit www.drtedzeff.com and go to the "Tips/Healing Insomnia" link.

Helping your HSB feel good about and in his body will help him to greet each new day with hope and energy. But the joy of living is not simply about physical well-being. Next, we'll look at your HSB's relationship to spirituality.

Spirituality and Self-Esteem

Jeffrey remembered, "I felt miserable that I didn't have any friends in elementary school and never fit in with the other kids. However, even as a boy I had some profound spiritual experiences that probably helped make me feel better about myself. I recall playing in my back-yard when I was about ten years old. Suddenly, my body froze and I entered into an altered state of consciousness. I knew that the house in front of me wasn't really my true home. In my heart I felt that I was from a different place, which was full of peace and harmony. I became completely detached from everyone and everything as a feeling of bliss permeated my body. After some time, I slowly returned to body consciousness. When I tried to explain this profound spiritual experience to my parents, they simply dismissed my experience, saying I must have had a dizzy spell. When I grew older and began reading about Eastern philosophy, I realized that that childhood experience was a glimpse into what is called nirvana or self-realization."

While your son's self-esteem may be diminished by his not fitting in with nonsensitive children, he will feel peaceful and worthwhile as he receives nourishment from his spiritual pursuits. Since all of the HSMs in my survey responded that throughout their life they have "always" or "usually" been intuitive, I've concluded that sensitive boys have a proclivity toward deep spiritual experiences.

Dan recalled, "From as far back as I can remember I was always interested in the meaning of life. When I was about six years old I remember standing in our kitchen as my mom prepared dinner and asking her how the Earth was created. Answering to the best of her ability, she said God made the world. The next question, of course, was where God came from. She simply responded that God has always been here. I remember that I couldn't grasp the concept of God's omnipresence, and I pondered how there could be no beginning or end. Even as a first grader, I remember being awestruck that there was something so big and omniscient that had always been here."

It would be beneficial to encourage your HSB to develop his spiritual side. Spirituality gives a feeling of stability and groundedness so that he won't be blown off center by challenging external situations (Paramatmananda, 2001). Brian described how a spiritual experience led to a profound positive change in his life as a young teenager: "I had a near-death experience when I was thirteen. I almost drowned, which actually turned out to be a gift. The experience heightened my spiritual sensitivities, and I became more empathetic toward other people. My near-death experience totally changed my life, and as a teenager I became interested in shamanic journeying from the Native American tradition, which I pursue to this day. I try not to let things bother me since I feel deeply connected to the Divine."

Similarly, Peter told me how spiritual experiences had had a positive impact on his life. "I think my first meditative experience happened when I took up running in middle school. Perhaps it was the endorphins being released when running, but I would get a spiritual high after my long runs.

"Then, when I was about fourteen, my uncle showed me how to meditate. Through doing regular meditation and deep-breathing techniques, I began experiencing more peace in my life as a new level of reality opened up to me. Even though my dad would frequently yell at me and put me down, I learned to watch my thoughts rather than immediately getting angry with him. It made me feel powerful and confident that I was able to not let his nasty behavior bother me!"

As HSBs move into early adulthood, spirituality continues to help them find peace and stability, as well as a stronger sense of their own value and purpose. Jonathan told me how developing his spiritual side has given him inner-peace. He said, "When I was in my early twenties I learned to accept my limitations, seeing my sensitivity as God's will. This has brought about a confidence level that I never had as a child or teenager. Meditation has helped me quiet my nervous system and emotional sensitivity. I wish I had learned to meditate when I was younger."

Likewise, Steve told me how his spiritual pursuits as a young adult have given him a great deal of peace of mind and increased his self-worth. "In my opinion, the purpose of life is to grow as a person by giving to others and connecting with God. Sensitive men seem to have an internal push to grow, and I have found that my religion appreciates sensitivity. In my value system, sensitivity is certainly the ideal that man is striving for. Instead of following the constant drumbeat of always seeking pleasure, my religious principles touch that part of my soul that tells me that life is about spiritual growth, so I push myself to become a better person.

"I think your self-esteem needs to be built up if you grow up as a sensitive boy in America, and I have done that with the help of my spiritual side. As a sensitive boy, sometimes people make fun of you, and as a teen, girls might not be that interested in you, so I ultimately found strength in my connection with God. If you follow a spiritual path then you are so much better off than those who are self-absorbed and very materialistic, which is what society at large seems to value. With a spiritual base, you can build a solid self-esteem that can remain with you for life."

How to Encourage Your HSB's Spirituality

Spending time in nature is an excellent way to develop your son's spirituality. The natural environment provides a space where he can easily awaken his innate divine qualities and where his sensitive nervous system has an opportunity to relax. Since the sensitive boy has the capacity to appreciate beauty deeply, he can easily enter into a tranquil state when he spends time in a safe, beautiful natural environment (Zeff, 2004).

Most of the HSMs in my study fondly recalled spending time in nature, where the quiet, beauty, and peace was the perfect antidote to our overstimulating world. Even boys who experienced a great deal of emotional pain during their childhood found peace in a natural environment. Terry recounted, "I fondly remember the joy I felt exploring the trails, creeks, and forest near my home. After sitting in a noisy classroom where I was sometimes teased, or having to endure the criticism, fighting, and screaming at home, I finally found deep peace in my nearby mystical and magical forest. There I could forget about all my troubles."

Ellen, a mother of a ten-year-old HSB named Zack, reported that her son suffered from low self-esteem as he tried to compete with the more aggressive boys in his school. No matter how often she told him that he had many wonderful qualities, Zack continuously negatively compared himself to his more extroverted peers. However, Ellen noticed that whenever the family went on a camping trip, Zack returned home full of peace and joy.

Take overnight camping trips, rent a cabin in the country, or go on day hikes with your HSB. You'll notice that he will thrive in the quiet, spacious environs of a magnificent, bucolic setting. You can also help your son enjoy nature around your house as you help him focus on a majestic tree in your backyard, the deep, green grass on the front lawn, and the crystal-clear azure sky above you.

Your son could also flourish in a Scouting environment provided that the Scout leaders are sensitive to his needs and the other children treat him kindly. It would also help his self-esteem to learn how to interact and work with other boys toward a common scouting goal.

Besides increasing your son's self-worth by introducing him to the tranquility of nature, you can help develop his spirituality by providing him with uplifting spiritual books to read. He may feel a kinship with such dharmic and divine heroes as Christ, Moses, Krishna, and Buddha, as well as the many saints and sages of all religions. Even if he doesn't fit in with other non-HSBs, he can find a feeling of connection to the compassionate spiritual heroes that uphold righteous values.

Another method to increase your son's inborn spirituality is to teach him meditation. Meditation focuses the attention on the breath or a mantra (repeating a word or words) while being a witness to the thoughts arising in the mind without reacting. This ancient practice helps calm down the nervous system and quiet the mind by lowering stress hormones in the body. It can also help your son sleep better, feel more grounded, and maintain a healthy body (Zeff, 1981). The following are some meditation books you could use to help your son learn this invaluable practice:

- *Teaching Meditation to Children: A Practical Guide to the Use and Benefits of Meditation Techniques* by David Fontana

- *Baby Buddhas: A Guide for Teaching Meditation to Children* by Lisa Desmond

- *Each Breath a Smile* by Sister Susan

Meditation is an excellent technique for managing the sensitive boy's stress and helping him stay in the present moment so that unpleasant experiences that he may have absorbed during the day can be flushed out.

While some young, sensitive boys may find it difficult sitting still, most boys could easily begin by watching their breath for a few moments. If your son has a positive experience with this short breathing exercise, you could try guiding your son through some of the relaxation exercises listed below. You can sit with him in a quiet, comfortable space and read him the exercises in a calm, gentle voice. Or, if you or your son prefers, you can make a recording of your voice (or someone else's) reading the exercises, which he can listen to anytime. While these exercises are more appropriate for the teenage and young-adult sensitive boy, younger HSBs may also benefit from the exercises.

Deep-Breathing Exercise

Sit in a comfortable position and close your eyes. Inhale slowly into your stomach to the count of five...hold to the count of five...and slowly exhale to the count of five...Visualize all the muscles in your body becoming more and more relaxed with each exhalation...

Repeat the slow deep-breathing exercise again...In for five...Hold for five...Out for five...Really experience how calm and peaceful your body feels with each exhalation...just observe any thoughts when they arise... then calmly return to your breathing...Inhale peace and calmness...hold... exhale any stress...

During the breathing exercise your HSB could also mentally repeat a mantra (such as the word peace or calm) with each inhalation and each exhalation. He may find it more comfortable to inhale to a count of fewer than five seconds. The timing of the breath should feel comfortable for him.

Progressive relaxation is another excellent way to calm your son's nervous system. This relaxation technique is performed by visualizing all of the muscles in the body relaxing more and more deeply. Your HSB may enjoy listening to the progressive-relaxation exercise on my

HSP Healing Program CD (available for purchase) or download at www. drtedzeff.com or listening to another relaxation tape.

Since your son is easily affected by other people's moods, it's important for him to learn to stay grounded. The following is an excellent visualization that you can read to your son, especially before or after school:

Centering Meditation

Once you have completed a few minutes of slow, deep breathing, imagine a green cord that is attached to the base of your spine Clearly observe the green cord The cord is slowly moving from your spine toward the floor Imagine two more green cords that are attached to the soles of your feet Now visualize all three green cords meeting at the Earth's surface and forming one large green cord

Observe this large green cord as gravity pulls the thick rope deeper toward the center of the Earth The cable is now traveling through layers and layers of solid rock deeper and deeper You can clearly see the cord traveling as it slowly sinks to the center of the Earth

Finally, the green cord arrives at the very center of the Earth The rope anchors itself to the Earth's center, and you begin to slowly inhale calm, centered, and stable energy from the Earth's core Visualize this energy slowly rising toward the Earth's surface with each inhalation

The energy easily rises towards the ground level Observe the grounding energy arrive at the Earth's surface The powerful energy ascends through the floor and into the soles of your feet You feel the energy rising up your legs You feel solid and centered, like a rock

Now feel the Earth's energy enter the base of your spine The serene, grounded energy feels so soothing Feel the Earth energy slowly travel up your spine and through your lower back mid back upper back neck all the way to the top of your head

You feel centered, calm, and strong as this core energy circulates throughout your entire being... filling every cell of your body...Breathe in the Earth's energy for a few moments...You are calm, centered, and

happy...You are calm, centered, and happy...You are calm, centered, and happy.

A helpful method to protect your son from negative energy coming at him from outside himself (such as other people's negative judgments or a bully's taunts) is for him to visualize a white light surrounding him. You can read this visualization to him whenever your son has to deal with a challenging situation, or you can suggest that he listen to a recording of it that you've made:

White-Light Meditation

Once you have completed a few minutes of slow, deep breathing, visualize a crystal-clear white light encircling your body Notice how the shimmering light encompasses every inch of your skin Observe clearly how strong the shield is Imagine negative energy bouncing off this impenetrable armor and ricocheting back to its source You are safe and protected You are safe and protected You are safe and protected.

Another spiritual method to increase your HSB's self-esteem is *hatha yoga*. Yoga postures consist of a series of stretching poses that tone the body while releasing stress. Yoga brings you into a natural state of tranquility by improving the endocrine metabolism, which reduces stress and stress-related disorders (Lad, 1984). You may want to enroll your son in a children's yoga class. Proper yoga instructors will advise your son to perform gentle movements and never to push himself into a pose.

The following are some yoga books that are beneficial for the young HSB:

- *Yoga for Children* by Mary Stewart

- *Create a Yoga Practice for Kids* by Yael and Matthew Calhoun

- *YogaKids: Educating the Whole Child Through Yoga* by Marsha Wenig

The following are some yoga DVDs for the young HSB:

- *Storytime Yoga: The Peddler's Dream*

- *Gaiam Kids: Yogakids Fun Collection*

- *Yoga for Families: Connect With Your Kid*

Conclusion

Being sensitive, your HSB tends to be more open to outside influences than non-HSBs. That is, he will often soak up messages and energy from those around him—both negative and positive. And, when he receives numerous negative messages and judgments (as is all too often the case), he can take these to heart, causing his self-esteem to sag. However, as a caring adult in his life, you have an enormous amount of power to counteract these messages and help your HSB hold on to the self-esteem he so richly deserves. By supporting him in his wonderful differences and unique qualities, you can help counteract messages he receives from the media, teachers, and peers that he's not okay. Teaching him to honor himself and giving him the skills to tap into his inner strength will instill in him the sense that he's doing just fine, just as he is. Next, we will discuss how to help your HSB deal with his emotional life.

Chapter 8

Living with Deep Emotions

"When our family moved from Atlanta to New York when I was twelve, I was emotionally devastated. I lost my best friend, my school, and my secret clubhouse in the woods. My parents didn't have a clue about the emotional pain I was going through."

"When my dad moved out when I was ten, he ended up remarrying and moving to another state, which was a huge loss for me. I remember becoming depressed and not wanting to go outside. Luckily, my mom sent me to a really good therapist, and after some time I was pretty much back to my old self."

As you well know, your HSB feels things deeply. Sometimes, this quality can mark him out as different and, to some, not masculine enough. In this chapter we will review how boys are taught to repress their emotions and how suppressing feelings negatively affects the sensitive boy. Then we will look into the emotional challenges that sensitive boys who have experienced difficult childhoods encounter. I'll offer many suggestions you can use to help your son improve his emotional life. And, if your HSB needs more advanced help, I'll offer a review of effective professional counseling modalities and information about how to choose the right counselor.

Boys Repress Their Emotions

Boys are taught from an early age not to express their emotions. As I mentioned in Chapter One, when boys express emotions such as fear, anxiety, or sadness, they are often seen as feminine and the adults around them typically treat them in ways that suggest that such emotions are not normal for a boy. While baby boys are actually more emotional than baby girls, by the age of five most boys suppress all their feelings except anger.

Since in most cultures the only acceptable male emotion to express is anger, there is a substantial amount of violence in the cruel culture of boys. Failing to fight when challenged is considered shameful for many boys and a sign that the boy is not masculine. Sensitive boys may experience fear more intensely than most boys, which can create severe anxiety when they are physically threatened.

One of the most distressing aspects of the rigid boy code is that males should never cry or express fear. The devastating effect of repressing emotions is demonstrated in male depression and suicide rates. Susan Nolen-Hoeksema at Stanford University found that boys aged eight to twelve were significantly more depressed than girls (Pollack, 1999). Even highly sensitive males avoid crying. While the research of Dr. Elaine Aron shows that men and women are equally divided in having the trait of high sensitivity, the only area where sensitive women scored significantly higher than sensitive men was in the statement, "I cry easily."

Males are also taught that it is a sign of weakness to ask for help. This follows logically from the pressure to suppress negative emotions besides anger; after all, if you are not supposed to have distressing emotions, why would you need help for them? The result is many men and boys who suffer in silence, which can have horrific effects for a male in his relationships, career, and health. I recently read the following quote at my local Veterans Administration hospital: "It takes the courage and strength of a warrior to ask for help. If you are in emotional crisis, contact the V.A. hospital." A real man needs to use his inner strength to shed years of media, familial, and societal brainwashing in order to be able to express his emotions and vulnerability.

Male Emotions and the Survival of the Planet

Repressing emotions and sensitivity have devastating effects on boys and men and the people who love them. But this expectation also has terrible consequences for the world at large. Males who repress their emotions have created a planet on the brink of disaster, since many male world leaders behave in a bellicose and combative manner rather than exhibiting compassionate and cooperative behavior. We are at a turning point for the planet in which our male political leaders can either continue acting in an insensitive, belligerent manner, risking the destruction of humanity, or choose a new, collaborative, understanding approach to foreign, economic, and environmental policy. By embracing the diversity of human experience—including masculine sensitivity—we can usher in a new era of world peace.

Reacting Strongly to a Troubled Childhood

Research by Dr. Elaine Aron indicated that the non-sensitive adults with troubled childhoods did not show nearly as much depression and anxiety as sensitive adults who experienced similar childhood trauma. However, highly sensitive people who had healthy childhoods are as emotionally well-adjusted as their non-HSPs counterparts (2002).

As we know, it's very difficult for sensitive boys to ignore teasing. Jerry remembered, "When I was teased at school for being one of the shortest boys in my class, I tried to ignore the taunting like my parents suggested, pretending that it didn't bother me. However, trying to ignore the teasing didn't help since I still deeply felt the emotional pain and the other kids could still tell that I was hurt."

Many sensitive boys who are emotionally or physically abused fail to tell anyone for fear of appearing weak or feeling shame that there's something wrong with them. Terry shared a sad tale of his discomfort about sharing his fears with anyone. "When I was about eight years old there were some rough and mean boys in my neighborhood who were after me. One day, my mother and I were getting out of the car and those boys approached and asked if I could play. My mom forced me to join them, even though I understood that their idea of 'playing' would be to terrorize me. Maybe she thought it would help me to try to make friends with those tough boys, but she clearly didn't realize how badly they would treat me.

"They took me to a nearby empty lot where they tied me up with a rope. Then the biggest boy yelled for another boy to get the knife. By this point, the adrenaline was soaring throughout my body, and since I knew I couldn't fight even one of them (let alone four boys), I somehow got the rope off and ran as fast as I could to my house. There was a wall on the front porch of the townhouse that jutted out about ten feet and was about two feet wide. I threw my body against the wall so the boys wouldn't see me. However, I knew that if my mom saw that I came home so soon she would scream at me for not playing with the neighbor boys.

"Speaking of being between a rock and a hard place! If I moved a few inches to the left the boys with the knife would come after me, and if I moved a few inches to the right my mother would get angry with me. Being up against the wall, I guess I learned that no matter where I go, I'm not safe. I've had chronic muscle tension throughout my life, and I always feel like I have to protect myself against potential danger. One therapist told me that I have post-traumatic stress syndrome from my horrifying childhood experiences. I wish that there had been someone I could have told about what happened to me, but I guess that I didn't want to look weaker than I already felt. I was so ashamed of myself, I just couldn't tell anyone what happened."

The Physiological Response to Stressful Events

While Terry's experience was unusually brutal, sensitive boys may experience emotional distress from such common occurrences as moving to a new house, changing schools, or losing a friend. During emotionally upsetting events, there is an excess of cortisol and a deficiency of serotonin in the body. An excess of stress hormones can create anxiety, apprehension, and fear. The stress hormones activate the central nervous system, leading to a habituated increase in muscle tension, heart rate, and blood pressure. An excess of cortisol also leads to increased vigilance and a restless mind. There is an exaggerated startle response, sounds appear louder, and lights seem brighter. During chronic stress, low levels of serotonin create a lack of feeling happy and fulfilled, which can lead to depression. Concurrently, the endorphins that create a sense of joy can literally dry up (Bhat, 1995).

When your son experiences severely upsetting situations, he could be at risk for developing *post-traumatic stress disorder* (PTSD), which is an anxiety disorder usually brought on by a terrifying physical or emotional event or events. Some of the symptoms of PTSD include sleep disturbances, withdrawal, a lack of concentration, and emotional numbness. Sometimes, when bullying reaches a point of serious physical threat (as Terry's did), the HSB's subsequent fear for his very life can bring on the symptoms of PTSD. And, because HSBs feel things so intensely, a situation that may not actually be life threatening may truly be *experienced* as life threatening to the HSB, resulting in similar trauma and emotional damage. The feeling of being out of control and in danger can cause the HSB to disconnect from others by isolating himself and experiencing hyperarousal and hypervigilance in a constant search for threats. This reaction is the nervous system's response to potential danger, whether real or imagined, creating constriction, disassociation, and helplessness in order to protect the body.

Unfortunately, when children experience trauma, they often become frozen and exhibit feelings of helplessness and shame, rendering them nearly unable to defend themselves when attacked or put under pressure. These traumatized children then bring this frozen state of helplessness to many other situations that they perceive as threatening throughout their lives (Levine, 1997). And, the more withdrawn these children become, the more fearful and helpless they feel, the stronger the likelihood that they will slip into serious emotional trouble.

Assessing the Emotional Damage

Parents, family members, teachers, and friends of our sensitive boys need to be aware of the warning signs their HSBs may be experiencing depression, severe anxiety, or PTSD. The following is a list of red flags to look for:

• Is your HSB disconnecting from people and isolating himself in his room? Although teens usually separate from the family, they normally connect more often with their friends.

• Has your HSB developed physical problems such as stomachaches and headaches that interfere with his life?

• Has your HSB's schoolwork recently suffered, and is it difficult for him to concentrate?

• Does your HSB have trouble falling or staying asleep? Does he experience frequent nightmares?

• Does your HSB seem listless, unenthusiastic, and disinterested in his life?

• Have you noticed that your HSB seems hypervigilant, extremely nervous, depressed, or emotionally explosive (beyond the normal teenage angst and moodiness)?

Help for Your HSB

If your son is experiencing any of the above symptoms, he needs increased one-to-one bonding with adults. His parents and the other adults in his life need to just listen to the HSB and be there for him in a nonjudgmental manner, letting him know that they love and support him.

Since sensitive boys feel emotions deeply, your son may ruminate about unpleasant experiences, so always point out your son's progress in other areas. If he keeps focusing on harmful experiences, he will create a habitual negative neural pattern in his brain that will be difficult to change. While the sensitive boy is still young, his parents need to help him develop a positive neuron pattern by replacing his negative thinking with new, positive thoughts. You can help your HSB create these positive neurological patterns by helping him focus on enjoyable experiences in the present moment. Once your son expresses his negative emotions, you can help him problem-solve solutions to his predicament, then have him engage in a favorite activity.

Professional Help

If you suspect that your son is suffering from severe emotional distress that is interfering with his life and you have not been able to help alleviate his suffering, you should consider having him evaluated by a licensed psychologist, licensed marriage and family counselor, or licensed social worker. If you can't afford to pay for private therapy sessions, virtually all cities have low-cost therapy clinics (check with your city or county department of mental health).

When choosing a counselor or therapist it's important to interview several carefully to determine which one is right for your son. You should inquire about the counselor's experience in working with sensitive boys and ask how they will create safety for your son in a therapeutic environment. Since every boy is different, the parents of an HSB need to determine if the potential therapist would be a good fit for their son. For instance, consider whether a male or female therapist would be better. In most cases I would recommend that boys see a male therapist who can serve as a supportive male role model. However, if the boy does not have a supportive adult female in his life, a female therapist could be the right choice.

Successful Counseling Modalities for the HSB

There are many different therapeutic methods to help the sensitive boy, so let's take a look at a few of the most effective.

Art and play therapy for the young HSB. The young sensitive boy (up to approximately age thirteen) should see a therapist who will engage in creative arts or play therapy, rather than just talking. The forced eye contact and the sedentary physical position in talk therapy can shut down your son's emotional and verbal centers, while physical activity can help promote emotional safety and emotional communication in boys. A boy feels safe and has an easier time accessing emotions when the therapist is doing some activity with him.

Creative arts and play therapy helps release negative emotions that sensitive boys absorb from other people. In addition, these therapeutic techniques help the child process unconscious inner conflicts. Art and play invite a child into the direct experience of inner knowing, following instincts, and even stimulating the body's innate balancing system (Crawford, 2009). Some of the modes of art and play therapy that your son could participate in are working with paints, crayons, clay, musical instruments, sand trays, puppets, and playing creative games.

Hakomi. Hakomi is a somatic-based therapy (body oriented) that is based on mindfulness, nonviolence, organicity, mind/body connection, and unity. Through mindfulness or awareness in the present moment, the client is able to safely access feelings and thoughts that lie deep within the body in a non-judgmental and non-violent atmosphere. The aspect of *organicity* means trusting and supporting the organic unfolding of the healing process in the body. The mind/body connection illustrates how emotions are mirrored in the body. And unity refers to a non-hierarchical therapeutic approach demonstrating the interconnectedness of all beings

In an e-mail to me, Will Sherwin, a therapist who has been trained in Hakomi, offered a great illustration of how integrating Hakomi with play therapy helped one shy, sensitive boy become more self-confident: "When children feel stuck behaving in ways that no longer work for them, I may use a puppet or stuffed animal to take over that behavior. I worked with Cory, a shy six-year-old boy who avoided contact with his classmates, rarely spoke at school, and did not assert himself. During our play sessions, I took the role of a snail puppet who was afraid and voiced fears every time Cory suggested something to do. The boy became curious and began reassuring the snail puppet. In a way, I was 'out-shying' him and giving him a chance to be the assertive one in the room. When he got a chance to exercise the assertive, risk-taking side of his character in our play sessions, he slowly began to take more risks in school. Taking over this child's behavior freed him to behave in a new, self-assured manner" (June 30, 2009).

Sports-oriented counseling. Some years ago, I worked at a family-service agency where I was the only male social worker. As the sole male therapist, I ended up seeing many boys for counseling. One mom, Esther, brought her shy, eleven-year-old son, Sean, to the agency. His presenting problem (the original reason they came in) was that Sean had no friends and would sit home alone after school and on weekends. To his mom, Sean seemed depressed. Esther, a single mom, said that Sean rarely saw his father who had remarried.

While playing a game with Sean during our first session, he mentioned that all the other guys in his class and neighborhood played football, but he didn't know how to play any sports. During our subsequent sessions, Sean and I would throw the football around as he opened up and told me how much he missed his dad and how lonely he felt.

Our "counseling" sessions also consisted of my showing Sean how to throw and catch a football. Once he learned the basics of handling the football, I showed him some new, cool plays. I enthusiastically encouraged him whenever he made a great catch or threw a perfect spiral pass. I still remember the huge smile that would light up his face whenever I complimented his athletic ability. Sean responded quickly to my encouragement and coaching. A short two months later he told me that he didn't want to hurt my feelings, but he would rather play with his friends after school instead of coming for counseling. The successful counseling sessions were concluded with a little encouragement, a supportive ear, and a football.

As you can see from this example, sometimes a shy, sensitive boy just needs the help of an older male to show him how to navigate through traditional boy activities. It also demonstrates the need for a therapist to be flexible in meeting a child's needs. Since each HSB is different, a competent counselor will need to carefully evaluate the most efficacious therapeutic approach for each client.

An innovative approach: Owning emotions. One innovative therapist, Barbara Schumer, a social worker who specializes in working with sensitive children, shared with me an interesting counseling approach she developed to prevent sensitive children from absorbing other people's energy. Barbara told me about a sensitive eleven-year old-boy, Jared, whom she had been seeing for counseling sessions for a few months. He would become extremely upset whenever his teacher disciplined other students in his class. Like a sponge, he would absorb the shame, guilt, and sadness of students who had misbehaved.

When Barbara met with Jared, she would ask him to notice when he began to take on other people's emotions. They would then track how he felt before and after absorbing other children's feelings. She created and played a game with Jared that she called, "Whose emotion is it anyway?" Jared would describe a scene from school as he visualized how he reacted to the incident. Then he would examine which emotions were his and which belonged to other children. By playing this game on a regular basis he became aware when he absorbed other people's energy. Over a period of a few months Jared was able to more easily set internal boundaries for himself and learn not to absorb other people's energy.

As a concerned parent, you could also work with your son to help him distinguish his emotions from those of others. That way, he won't be so affected by other people's moods and feelings. You could try the game I mentioned in the example above. That story also illustrates how important it is for a therapist to utilize creative approaches when working with the sensitive child. When interviewing a potential counselor for your son, it's important to find out what specific techniques he or she will be using. And don't be reticent in making suggestions to the therapist about techniques that you feel will be most effective for your son.

A Harmful Therapeutic Experience

If you do not thoroughly screen a potential therapist, a potentially therapeutic experience could actually be detrimental for your sensitive boy. Steve told me that when he was going through an emotionally traumatic time being taunted by other children in seventh grade, his parents sent him to a psychologist. Steve remembered, "That old-fashioned psychologist made me feel like it was my fault for being teased. When Dr. Gold asked me why the kids were taunting me, I naturally responded, 'I don't know.' I refused to talk to him since I was embarrassed about being humiliated at school and that incompetent therapist didn't have a clue why I wouldn't answer his questions. Like a twelve-year old boy is going to tell a stranger why he's being teased.

"It was agony for me to have put up with his relentless inquires about why I misbehaved at home. Of course I was having temper tantrums at home after being humiliated all day at school, but Dr. Gold never acknowledged the pain I was dealing with. I used to be afraid that people would think I was crazy if they saw me walking into that psychologist's office, which was another reason why I never wanted to go to those terrible sessions. To top it all off, my mother would criticize me for not talking to Dr. Gold and tell me that I was wasting my father's hard-earned money. Gee, more guilt—just what I needed. As though I didn't feel bad enough about myself as it was."

Finding the right child therapist. As you can see from Steve's horrific therapeutic experience, it's crucial for parents to find a skilled therapist for their child. Be sure to carefully screen and monitor any potential therapist.

While most children under thirteen would be uncomfortable talking to a therapist, some mature eleven- or twelve-year-olds may easily be able to sustain a conversation about themselves. Conversely, some thirteen- or fourteen-year-olds may not feel comfortable opening up to adults. However, a skilled therapist with experience working with adolescents can find innovative ways to engage them.
Some important points to consider when choosing and monitoring a child therapist:

- Ask your doctor, school counselor, or friends for names of excellent child therapists whom they trust and recommend.

- Ask the potential therapist about his or her experience working with sensitive boys and how they would work with the child and family.

- Find out whether you can attend the first session to observe how the therapist interacts with your child.

- Let your HSB know before the first session that you want him to feel comfortable with the therapist.

Regularly ask your son if he feels comfortable, safe, and valued when meeting with his therapist and observe how willing your son is to attend sessions. Is the therapist responsive to your concerns about treatment, and is your son getting better?

Therapy for the Teenage HSB

The sensitive male has the right attributes for emotional healing, regardless of his age. So, if your HSB is in his teenage years, he can still benefit tremendously if you help him get the counseling he may need. Sensitive males are intuitive, have access to their unconscious mind, and have a rich inner life. They also exhibit curiosity, integrity, and understanding. In a loving and accepting therapeutic relationship, the sensitive teenage male can flourish.

Dan had a life-changing, positive experience with his therapist when he was in high school. He fondly recalled, "When I was sixteen, my parents thought there was something wrong with me and sent me to a therapist. Mr. Klern was a sensitive man who became a male role model for me, showing me that it's okay to express my feelings. He totally supported my sensitivity, letting me know that aggressive kids who made fun of gentle boys were clearly wrong, and he helped me learn the value of feeling and expressing my emotions. Mr. Klern probably saved my life. He gave me the strength to be who I am."

Dan's beneficial therapeutic experience illustrates how valuable it is for a sensitive adolescent boy to see an HSM therapist who can serve as a role model, validating that it's okay for sensitive boys to express their feelings. However, even a non-HSP therapist who is supportive and nonjudgmental is a godsend for the HSB suffering from low self-esteem.

Finding the right therapist for an adolescent. Parents of teenage HSBs should consider the following points when choosing and monitoring a therapist for their son:

- Ask your doctor, school counselor, or friends for names of excellent therapists who have experience working with adolescents.

- Ask the potential therapist if they regularly work with sensitive teenage boys.

- Tell the therapist what is happening with your teen and closely observe their response to see if it fits with the developmental issues your son is dealing with.

• Ask the therapist how they handle confidentiality and their proto-
col for talking to parents.

• After interviewing therapists with your son, let him choose the
therapist he feels most comfortable with.

• Monitor how comfortable your son is during the therapy sessions.
If your son wants to quit, it's important for him to discuss his reasons with the therapist before immediately ending treatment.

• If you sense that your son feels devalued, unsafe, or uncomfortable,
discuss how he can resolve these feelings with the therapist. If this
tactic is unsuccessful or you feel that your HSB is in danger of having a negative experience, end treatment and find a new therapist.

The Young-Adult Male Choosing a Therapist

When the young adult HSM is choosing a counselor or therapist it's
also important to interview several potential therapists carefully to
determine which one feels right. As an adult, he will most likely be
searching for a therapist on his own. However, you can still offer assistance by providing some names of therapists and letting him read this
information about finding the right counselor.

Your young HSM will probably be choosing among various treatment modalities (for instance, cognitive-behavioral therapy, Jungian
therapy, somatic, and so on), but he will also need to determine how
empathetic the therapists are towards HSMs. He should formulate some
good questions of his own and listen carefully for both knowledge
about and support of the trait of sensitivity from the potential therapist
(Zeff, 2004).

There are a variety of healing modalities to consider before decid-
ing on a counselor or therapist. For short-term counseling, seeing a
cognitive-behavioral therapist would be appropriate. This treatment
modality will teach your HSM specific practical and rational approaches

for dealing with his current situation. For longer-term therapy to deal with deeper emotional issues, other modalities such as Freudian, Jungian, Gestalt, Rogerian, or client-centered approaches usually work more effectively. Finally, a somatic or body-oriented approach can be helpful in teaching the HSM to release emotions stored up in his body. Some examples of somatic-based therapies include Bioenergetics, Reichian, and Hakomi. The HSM may be able to find a therapist experienced in more than one of these modalities.

Each HSM is unique. A method that helps one young man could actually have an adverse effect on another. Each sensitive young man needs to carefully review the various therapeutic modalities and use his intuition to choose the therapy that is best for him. In *The Highly Sensitive Person's Survival Guide*, I've included a chapter on choosing an appropriate healer. Also, Elaine Aron's *The Highly Sensitive Person* offers a very informative chapter that succinctly describes various counseling and therapeutic options to consider.

The HSM may also want to participate in a supportive group-therapy program. Although group therapy can be a beneficial process, some HSMs may feel overwhelmed, shy, or uncomfortable in a group setting. A group should have a sufficient number of HSPs and the facilitator needs to be very supportive and skilled in working with HSPs in a group setting. You may want to follow Elaine Aron's model in *The Highly Sensitive Person's Workbook* for starting your own HSP discussion group.

Conclusion

As you know, your HSB or HSM feels things deeply. This means he has the opportunity for great joy, creativity, and compassion, which you've probably already witnessed in his life. However, this sensitivity can also mean that he feels pain, sadness, and anger more intensely than others, sometimes resulting in lingering trauma and a lack of confidence.

Fortunately, there is help available. As always, your love and understanding can salve some of these wounds, demonstrating that your son is not alone in his feelings and can count on you for support. And, as many sensitive and non-sensitive people do, an HSB or HSM can benefit from professional help, learning more about himself and gaining specific skills to help him live his life in a manner that truly meets his needs.

Next we will look into the world of the teenage and young-adult sensitive male and investigate many coping strategies that will help make the sensitive boy's transition to manhood easier.

Chapter 9

The Sensitive Teenage Boy and Young Adult

"When I was younger I used to feel that women didn't want to date me because they thought I was too sensitive and not tough enough. However, my wife regularly expresses her appreciation for my sensitivity, which has been a big boost to my self-esteem. It's so important for sensitive men to choose partners who support their temperament."

"My first job was working as a salesman on a commission basis. I couldn't stand the intense pressure, knowing that I wouldn't get paid if I didn't make a sale. I just didn't have the personality for that job, and after a few months, I quit. I then got a salaried job working in a small art-supply store. I really enjoyed the more-relaxed and artistically oriented atmosphere. "

In this chapter we will discuss some of the distinctive challenges facing the sensitive teenage and young-adult male, including dating and school. We'll look at rites of passage from boyhood to manhood for the sensitive young man, and I'll offer some practical coping strategies for the HSM entering college and the world of work.

Welcome to the Stimulating World of Teenagers

When your HSB was young, he may have spent much of his time alone at home or with only one other friend pursuing quiet activities. Therefore, you may be surprised if your newly teenaged HSB starts taking part in activities that seem uncharacteristic for a sensitive boy. This new behavior by some HSBs is the result of a higher tolerance for stimulation shown by many sensitive teenagers, who are able to withstand (and even enjoy) stimulation that would probably overwhelm the typical younger HSB or older HSM. Some sensitive teenagers can tolerate listening to loud music and partying to all hours of the night. I am extremely noise sensitive and look back in wonder as to how I used to regularly tolerate attending raucous, noisy parties during my teenage years. However, even if the teenage sensitive boy pursues a more stimulating lifestyle, he still needs more downtime than his non-HSB counterpart or he may suffer from nervousness and fatigue.

The sensitive teenager needs to find the right balance between engaging in too many or too few activities. During adolescence, when your HSB is trying to become independent, it's essential for adults to remain available to support and encourage him. For example, you could suggest to your son that that he doesn't have to keep up an intense schedule like his non-HSP peers. Instead, he can choose to spend time with other sensitive teens in a quiet setting or pursue social connections in the calmer environment of the Internet. Although some teenage boys may initially appear resistant to receiving affection from parents, if your son is open to it, you can show your support through giving a goodnight hug and telling your son that you love him. I think that sensitive teenage boys would really enjoy receiving such love from their parents even if they aren't always able to show it.

Dating

Sensitive teenage boys may feel very insecure when they begin to date since many may be shy or believe that their sensitivity is not so appealing to girls. Being in a close relationship can be challenging, since sensitive males feel emotions more deeply and fall in love with more intensity than non-HSBs.

Your son needs to learn that it's okay to set boundaries when he's in a relationship, rather than feeling that he has to play the role of the strong man who can handle everything. He should date people who understand and accept his sensitivity, instead of being with a partner who pressures him to act differently.

Dating Girls in High School

Ryan reported, "As a teenager I saw my sensitivity as a drawback, since I didn't feel like I measured up to the image of the strong, confident, extroverted man. I found that some girls were not attracted to sensitive guys—usually because they were looking for a stereotypical type of guy who acted tough and assertive. However, now that I'm older, I feel that my sensitivity is actually an advantage when meeting women since I think that I appear more mature than the average guy. I also feel that women like the fact that I'm good at talking about feelings and understanding what they need."

Author Terry Kupers has clearly stated some of the challenges for the dating high-school-age sensitive boy. "Sensitive men often have trouble as teenagers since frequently high school culture values tough guys. But later, as an adult, sensitivity can turn out to be a valuable asset when women are able to value it in a way they were not able to in high school. When girls get older they might figure out it's much better to be involved with a man who can be sensitive to their needs. The challenge for a sensitive male is to weather the high school years and not give up his sensitivity; then later, that sensitivity is one of the things others will find most lovable about him" (1993).

Successful Relationships for the Sensitive Young Man

Since young people tend to have less self-knowledge and less discrimination, the teenage HSB may choose a partner based solely on physical attractiveness or social status. However, if the HSB doesn't consider a potential partner's temperament or their understanding and acceptance of male sensitivity, the young sensitive man could end up in an uncomfortable relationship. Parents should discuss these important aspects of dating with their teenage HSB.

Some HSMs reported that their girlfriends thought there was something wrong with them for not wanting to go out so much. Joel reported, "When I was in my early twenties I had a girlfriend who was critical of me for not wanting to go to noisy parties or to crowded bars and restaurants. Since I was the only one of our friends who didn't like to go out, I not only felt bad about myself, but I ended up getting into a lot of arguments with my girlfriend."

Doug described his experiences with two women: "My first girlfriend was an extrovert, and she was always demanding that I take part in her favorite activities. She enjoyed rock climbing, but I never felt comfortable with that risky sport. My hesitance to participate made me feel like I wasn't a real man. The truth is that I'm a little scared of heights, which I could never admit to that girlfriend. Instead of being honest, I would make up excuses about why I didn't want to go rock climbing. She probably didn't believe my excuses, which created a strain on the relationship. We ended up fighting all the time until we finally broke up.

"My current girlfriend is sensitive, but not highly sensitive. She's an easy person to be with and allows me the space to be who I am. She seems to intuitively know when I need support and when I need to be left alone. I think we get along so well since I can be myself with her."

Steve also told me about the advantages of choosing women who can appreciate his sensitivity. "When I was younger I was confused about girls. Though I'm attractive, I think that some girls I was interested in at the time didn't want to date me because I was too nice. Luckily, as I got older, I found more mature women who appreciated my kindness and sensitivity, and the issue became less relevant. I have a great relationship with my wife because I articulate my feelings well and can empathize with her, probably better than most men could."

Sensitive males need to learn to compromise and communicate clearly if they are in a relationship with a non-highly sensitive partner. For example, if there is a disagreement about attending a noisy party, the partners could find the middle ground by stopping by for a short time rather than staying for hours. Sometimes an HSM's partner may feel rejected when he wants to spend time alone. Therefore, he needs to reassure his partner that he is not avoiding her and let her know exactly how much downtime he needs. Both partners have to be flexible in order to create optimal levels of interaction and employ creative solutions. Couples need to learn to accept each other's differences rather than blaming each other for having a different temperament.

If a sensitive male is in a relationship with a sensitive partner, the advantage is that she will understand him and will also probably want to spend time alone. This similarity can create safety in the relationship. However, some difficulties may be compounded when both partners have challenges about going out in the world (Aron, 2001). For more information about sensitive people in relationships, I recommend reading Dr. Elaine Aron's book, *The Highly Sensitive Person in Love* (2001).

Sensitive Men Make Better Lovers

Contrary to the media stereotype that women crave macho men who are tough, silent, and unemotional, sensitive men have extraordinary appeal for women. Sensitive men are not only more tuned into their own needs but to the needs of their partners.

Older teenage and young-adult sensitive males shouldn't feel pressured to have a sexual relationship before it feels right to them, which contradicts the myth that men want sex all the time. However, when the sensitive man is ready for a sexual relationship, he has a distinct advantage. Gary pointed out, "I think that my sensitivity only enhances my ability to empathize with women. As for sexuality, I'm able to be sensitive to the needs and the pleasure of what my wife wants. When

I can appreciate the pleasure of someone else, it enhances my own pleasure."

Brian stated, "Since I didn't fit the cultural stereotype of masculinity, I risked being viewed as effeminate. However, as a sensitive man I've probably been more sensitive to my sexual partner's needs throughout my life than most men. I feel at ease with women sexually, comfortably giving and receiving physical contact such as hugs and touching. So, sensitive men probably make better lovers."

Rites of Passage for Sensitive Boys

All boys need to learn the proper balance between assertive and gentle behavior to successfully function as a man. Sensitive boys need to learn how to assert themselves to survive in our aggressive world, while non-HSBs need to learn how to express their feelings and vulnerability in order to have successful interpersonal relationships.

Nowadays, we've lost many of the traditional practices that helped mark passages in life. For instance, one of the reasons gangs have increased in the last fifty years is because males are looking for ways to be initiated into manhood, lacking the initiation rituals of ancient times (Gurian, 2007). However, the more acceptable current rites of passage for young men such as joining the military or a college fraternity may not be appropriate for the sensitive teenage or young-adult male.

The initiation into teen peer culture frequently includes humiliation, where the humiliated newcomer is expected to regain his sense of composure, then turn around and join other boys in humiliating the next newcomers (Kupers, 1993). I remember tolerating the humiliation and frustration of pledging a college fraternity when I attended Rutgers University many years ago. The callous and ruthless conditions I experienced pledging a fraternity created severe stress for my sensitive nervous system. The fear and angst that I experienced may have canceled out any benefits that I gained when I was finally initiated into the group of young men. Even as a fraternity member, I knew that I was different than most of the other guys when I watched from the sidelines as they played aggressive football games or observed the way they would talk about and behave crudely toward young women.

The sensitive young man needs to be supported in his transition into manhood by his immediate and extended family, as well as by members of the community. The initiation into manhood for the intuitive and spiritual teenage boy may involve being exposed to archetypical and mythological stories told by elder males. Also, every spiritual tradition has meaningful stories that can help the sensitive teenage male learn about morality, virtue, and justice. Through being exposed to stories about spiritual heroes, the sensitive young man will discover what it means to be a strong, sensitive, and compassionate man.

Historically, indigenous tribes have often recognized the sensitive boy as someone with special healing powers, and the elder males would initiate him into being a shaman. Likewise, you could find responsible elder males who could initiate your sensitive son into manhood by creating a special ceremony tailored for him. Through participation in religious and spiritual ceremonies or through mentoring by elder males, the sensitive young man can experience a gentle initiation into manhood. This spiritual awakening is a vital component of his initiation into manhood.

College

For some sensitive males it may be better to attend a local college and live at home rather than going away to college right out of high school, since major life changes can be challenging for the HSM. Some sensitive young men may become anxious and stressed as they simultaneously try to adjust to living in a noisy college dorm and cope with the pressures of a new, rigorous academic environment. Therefore, making a slow transition to college would likely be less stressful for the sensitive young man.

A significant number of college students, both highly sensitive and non-highly sensitive, have difficulty adjusting to living away from home their freshman year and end up dropping out of school. I'm grateful that I ended up living at home and commuting to a local college, rather than going away to school when I was eighteen. In retrospect, I realize that I probably wouldn't have been able to handle the stress of living in a noisy dormitory and coping with all the pressures of adjusting to a new academic environment.

The Sensitive Male at Work

The teenage and young-adult sensitive male should consider the following factors before pursuing employment: Sensitive people tend to work best in a quiet, calm, and supportive environment, and they often find it difficult to work under time pressure. They have a very challenging time working for an insensitive, demanding boss or with difficult colleagues. The HSM's supervisor needs to understand that he or she will get much better results by allowing the sensitive male to process information slowly, rather than pressuring him to produce answers quickly. The quality of work the HSM can produce will be thoughtful and excellently done if he can work in conditions that meet his needs.

The feeling of not being able to live up to non-highly sensitive, Type A work standards can create frustration, anxiety, and low self-esteem for the sensitive young man. He needs to accept his work limitations and not compare himself with others. The sensitive young man needs a lot of downtime and may find it difficult to work a forty-hour-plus week. He should also carefully evaluate the physical environment in terms of noise, lighting, odors and stimulation. However, when he can work in conditions that suit his sensitivity, the HSM often produces better quality work due to his careful, creative, and conscientious temperament.

The sensitive young man needs to take these points into consideration before he embarks on a specific career, or even before taking a summer or part-time job. I remember feeling overwhelmed and anxious when I was a waiter at a summer overnight camp in high school. I had a very critical and demanding boss, and I became quite nervous trying to responsibly fulfill all my duties under such pressure.

When considering a profession, the HSM should also take into consideration the positive attributes of his temperament. Joel, an information-technology consultant, said that his natural tendency to pause and reflect while problem solving is respected by his colleagues. Similarly, those in the helping professions admire the empathetic sensitive male, and people in the artistic community highly regard the sensitive man's creativity.

HSMs make excellent employees since they tend to be creative, conscientious, thoughtful, and loyal. They tend to socialize less with others, often preferring to process experiences quietly by themselves. They notice subtleties in the work environment and frequently come up with innovative solutions at work. Once the sensitive young man finds the right job and feels that there is a purpose to his work, he becomes an exceptional employee.

What Job Is Suitable for the Sensitive Male?

The thirty highly sensitive men that I interviewed had a variety of jobs, with each man possessing different interests, abilities, and talents. These sensitive men worked in many different professions, including as a physician, attorney, social worker, website designer, teacher, small-business owner, and electrician.

Several men discussed how difficult it was for them to work in a competitive work environment. Brian, an accountant from Denver, told me about his experiences working in a managerial position in the corporate world: "I was in a stressful management position for many years, and although I was successful, I disliked my demanding job. I suppose I didn't quit because of the 'golden handcuffs,' and because I was unwilling to admit to myself that the job was too stressful for my temperament. Competing with other men under intense pressure ended up destroying my health. I began suffering from insomnia, gastrointestinal problems, and I developed a hand tremor.

"I would see things that were unfair at work, but I knew that if I spoke up I could lose my job. It was so difficult for me, as a sensitive and caring man, to continue to accept such flagrant unfairness. Most employers didn't appreciate my awareness and didn't want 'to fix what isn't broken.' My altruistic tendencies created a lot of problems when I worked in such a rigid environment. In the cutthroat corporate world not only was I passed by for promotion, but I was afraid that I would be fired if I informed my boss that I was sensitive and needed special accommodations.

"Finally I couldn't take it anymore, so I started my own business as an accountant, working by myself, which has been fantastic. I have a quiet and comfortable office with a magnificent view of the mountains. I don't have to interact with many people since I do a lot of my work on the computer. Although I'm earning less money than when I worked for a large corporation, I would much rather have peace of mind than the extra cash."

Lars, a psychologist from Denmark, made an interesting point about sensitive men in Danish society. "In Denmark I have found that sensitive men are accepted and honored in professions dominated by women but not recognized or admired in professions dominated by men." Likewise, in the United States, I spent some time as the sole male therapist working in a small family-services agency. My female colleagues were extremely appreciative to have a man who could work with male clients. Sensitive men tend to advance to supervisory roles quicker in professions dominated by women than in the male-dominated corporate world, as Brian noted.

Jeffrey, a social worker from Chicago, also experienced the pitfalls of working in an all-male environment. "I used to work in a group home with angry, testosterone-laden adolescent boys, which was probably the worst environment for a sensitive man to work in. I was frequently verbally assaulted and threatened by enraged, macho teenage boys, yet I think I secretly wanted those tough boys to respect me, so I didn't quit the thankless job. Finally, the funding for the group home ended, and I was (thankfully) laid off. I feel that no one, especially a sensitive male, should have to work in such an abusive environment. I now work as an administrator for a mental-health agency, which I enjoy."

As with so many aspects of being highly sensitive in this non-highly sensitive world, it's important for the HSM is to find a professional life that meets his needs. Though he may experience quite a lot of pressure to honor only his economic needs or to prove himself in a tough, back-biting profession, he needs to look at what will make him happy. When the HSM honors his needs and his temperament, he will produce better-quality work and can lead a more joyful and productive life.

Investigating Various Job Possibilities

One way for the sensitive young man to decide if a job is right for him is to volunteer in that particular field. Volunteering is an excellent way to learn about a job and obtain experience that could lead to a paid job in the future. Another option is to begin working part time in an entry-level position to determine if the job is suited to his temperament. For example, a student may want to take a summer job as a counselor at a day camp to determine if he is suited to working with children; or, he could try working as a messenger for a law firm to get a rudimentary understanding of life in the legal world.

The sensitive young man could do his own labor-market survey, asking employers about current hiring levels, salary, qualifications, as well as the physical and emotional demands of the types of jobs he's interested in. It's crucial to realistically evaluate if any potential job is suitable for the sensitive male's temperament. Elaine Aron's informative chapter on thriving at work in her book *The Highly Sensitive Person* (1996) has many additional tips to help the HSM find suitable employment (as well as an excellent summary of tips for employers of sensitive people in the back of her book).

Self-Employment

Many of the HSMs in my survey expressed a desire to work for themselves to avoid the negative effects of working with an autocratic supervisor, difficult coworkers, or in an inhospitable environment. However, young sensitive males should be realistic when investigating the possibility of self-employment. According to Dr. Aron, "Self-employment is a logical route for HSPs. You control the hours, the stimulation, the kinds of people you deal with, and there are no hassles with supervisors or coworkers. However, you have to be careful about being a perfectionist, driving yourself too hard, and you need to be willing to make difficult decisions. Also, you need to be careful not to isolate yourself too much. If you work alone, it's important to meet with colleagues regularly for support. Introverted sensitive people could also have some challenges with the marketing aspect of self-employment" (1996).

Tom, a small-business owner from Rhode Island, told me, "I knew even when I was a teenager that I couldn't tolerate working for others in a noisy environment and that I would have to create my own safe haven for work. I've been successfully self-employed for twenty-nine years and love it. Self-employment has been a blessing in my life."

Like Tom, I have thrived when I've worked for myself. Many years ago I worked for a large private company, which I found extremely stressful. I had to share an office with a colleague who talked loudly on the phone, and I needed to meet a requirement of billable hours each week. Since I quit that job, I've been happily self-employed as a private counselor and writer for most of my life, working in a quiet office and creating my own daily schedule.

Conclusion

Making the transition from boyhood to manhood can be difficult for every male. For the highly sensitive male, this transition poses special challenges, as the boy works out what it means to be a sensitive man.

As your HSB moves toward manhood, remember that your support will be crucial. Allow him to make his own choices (and possibly, mistakes) while reminding him that you will be there to help, if needed. Also, if your HSM loses his way on his life's journey, you can gently remind him of his positive qualities and that he needs to honor his temperament. While a young man will want to establish his independence, he will benefit by knowing that you're there to support him when he needs it.

Next we'll look at some revealing questions and answers about and from HSBs, HSMs, and the people who love them.

Chapter 10

Questions and Answers

This chapter is a bit different from the others in *The Strong, Sensitive Boy*. Here we'll be looking at questions I've received over my professional life from parents of sensitive boys and sensitive young men, followed by my direct answers. While every question may not directly apply to your HSB right now, this chapter will help you learn more about challenges and solutions for the sensitive boy and young adult male. You may find some of the information more helpful as your HSB grows and changes, so I suggest you read it in its entirety and come back to it when new situations arise. I've structured the chapter to be in a question-answer format, which will make it easier to refer back to questions of interest to you. As you read, it may be helpful to make notes of the answers that you would like to integrate into your life.

Question: *My shy younger son is not interested in sports and prefers to stay home after school and weekends, watching TV or playing games on his computer by himself. This behavior is unlike his older brother's, who participates in many sports regularly with his friends. I feel that my younger boy is unhappy always being alone. How much should I push him to participate in sports, which will probably help him make new friends* *so he isn't by himself all the time? Wouldn't it be good for him to interact with his peers instead of just with his family?*

Answer: My study indicated that eighty-five percent of sensitive boys did not participate in team sports and reported that, throughout their lives, they preferred to participate in individual exercise. Sensitive boys tend to shy away from group sports since they do not perform well under group pressure and may be deeply hurt by the cruel culture of boy teasing while playing sports. However, I found that the more athletically inclined sensitive boys tended to have happier childhoods than those who did not participate in team sports as a boy.

Is there any team sport that your son is interested in? If so, you could talk with the coach and other parents to make sure that the players are treated with respect and are not overly competitive so that your son can feel comfortable participating. While involvement in team sports could be helpful for your son in order to learn how to navigate through the aggressive, competitive world of boys, don't push him to participate if he shows no interest. However, your son should engage in some daily physical activity. He and other family members could engage in individually oriented physical activities together, such as bike riding, swimming, or hiking.

Question: *I am a highly sensitive man who is attending college, majoring in pre-med. Even though I've always been interested in the healing professions and get top grades, I think that it might be too stressful for me to attend medical school and work as a physician. My parents are encouraging me to go on to medical school, but I'm worried that I might not make it through the academic, residency, and internship program.*

Answer: I remember one HSM client told me that when he was a surgical resident he was totally stressed out. Most sensitive people like to pause and reflect before acting, and as a resident in a busy hospital, this client said that he couldn't think quickly enough on his feet. However, once he completed his residency and eventually opened his own private practice, he felt calmer. The ability to set his own schedule allowed him to include the downtime he needed. Also, his private practice enabled him to connect emotionally with his patients, which he was virtually unable to do in the institutional setting of a hospital. While you will likely experience some stress during your medical training, once you're a physician you can create the time and space you need to treat each patient in the way that feels comfortable. It would help to read *The Highly Sensitive Person's Survival Guide* (2004) to learn how an HSM can successfully deal with the stress that you will encounter during your medical training. The world certainly needs more sensitive physicians.

Question: *I'm a mom of a twelve-year-old boy, and I have a very big problem with my son. I'm worried that my son may be gay. He's hyper-sensitive about everything and acts in a very emotional way, still crying when he gets upset. He prefers feminine activities like cooking, and he still plays with stuffed animals and toy cars. That behavior just doesn't seem natural to me, and his dad is always bugging him to act more like a real boy. What can I do to help him get over his sensitivity and make sure he turns out normal?*

Answer: First of all, just because your son is sensitive and emotional does not mean that he is gay. Many of the greatest chefs in the world are men and maybe he enjoys playing with his stuffed animals because he's seeking more love and nurturance in his life. My initial research indicated that ninety-five percent of the HSMs in my survey are hetero-sexual. There is no proven correlation between males with a finely tuned nervous system and homosexuality.

Unfortunately, our society frequently equates sensitive males with homosexuality, and there is a misperception that most gay males are highly sensitive. There is no data to support the belief that most gay males have a finely tuned nervous system. However, even if your son turns out to be gay, he will need special love and support from you and your husband, extended family members, teachers, and the entire community to counteract the negative societal stigma toward homosexuality.

Your son is behaving normally for a sensitive boy. You may want to consider that society's misperception of what constitutes masculine behavior is the real problem. It would help your son if you and your husband examine how you developed your belief system about how a boy should act and consider whether your beliefs are increasing or decreasing your son's self-esteem and sense of self-worth. One wise spiritual teacher has said, "It is no measure of health to be well-adjusted to a profoundly sick society."

Question: *I have noticed that when my seven-year-old son is playing with other boys, he allows them to dominate him. He seems to put up with other kids being mean to him and doesn't speak up. He doesn't even fight back when he's been pushed. I'm concerned that he may get bullied if he doesn't learn to assert himself. I'm not sure how to handle the situation.*

Answer: It's good that you are aware of your son's experience and want to help him prevent domination and abuse by aggressive children. Other children may perceive HSBs as different, and since bullies target people who stand out, sensitive boys are more vulnerable to bullying. Many victims of bullies are reluctant to defend themselves or retaliate, and sensitive boys become more upset when teased than other boys, which is likely to intensify the abuse.

It would be helpful for you to teach your son how to respond to aggressive children by role-playing with him. Help him practice looking the other child in the eye and saying, "If you can't play with me in a respectful way, I want you to back off now." You may also want to read books about how to deal with bullies, such as *The Everything Parents Guide to Dealing with Bullies* by Deborah Carpenter (2009). Also, your HSB can learn how to defend himself by taking a class in some form of self-defense. Your help and the techniques I've offered can give your son the self-confidence to be able to stand up for himself. And remember, it's critical that you nip the problem in the bud while he's still young.

Question: *I'm the single mom of an eight-year-old boy named Connor. Since my husband left me four years ago, it's been just the two of us.*

Connor's dad remarried and rarely sees him. Recently, a male friend of mine commented that my son and I seemed more like a couple than parent and child. He said that he felt like a third wheel when he visited me. That comment still really bothers me, and I'm wondering if I'm depending on my son too much to meet some of my own needs.

Answer: It's great that you were able to hear your friend's comment and not discount it out of hand. It may be the impetus you need to work toward getting the support you and your son really need.

Parenting can be tough, and a single mom especially needs a support network of family, friends, neighbors, and members of the community to help her raise her son. It would be helpful for you to find male role models for your son to spend time with. Does he have a grandfather, uncle, or older male cousin that he could get together with? Is the male friend you mentioned interested in mentoring your son? There are reputable mentoring and Big Brothers programs that have helped tens of thousands of boys. But this dynamic your friend spoke of isn't just about your son—it's also about you. As the adult, it's your responsibility to get your emotional needs met without depending on your son. Just like when you hear a flight attendant tell you to put the air mask over your face before attending to your child, you will need to take care of yourself in order to take better care of your son. Go ahead and develop your interests by taking a class or joining a group that's involved in interesting new activities. You may want to see a counselor or therapist to help you create a healthier, less-dependent relationship with your son, or join a group of single moms who are dealing with similar issues. Give yourself the permission to take care of you so your son doesn't have to bear that responsibility

Question: My husband and I both need to work full-time to make ends meet. When my daughter, Sarah, was three years old, I went back to work. Sarah didn't seem to mind when I had to leave her at preschool, and I think the interaction she had with the other children has been good for her development. Although the preschool has many children, there is a good teacher-student ratio. Sarah is now in first grade and is doing well.

However, when I tried to put my three-year-old son, Bobby, in the same child-care center a few weeks ago, he totally freaked out. Bobby wouldn't stop crying when I left him, and the preschool director is at a loss as to how to handle him. I'm really stuck, since we can't live on just my husband's salary, yet I'm worried about how upset Bobby becomes whenever I leave him to go to work.

Answer: It sounds like your daughter is probably not as sensitive as your son. The highly sensitive child frequently feels overwhelmed when he enters a strange, noisy, overstimulating environment. If Bobby becomes so upset when you leave him, it is a sign that you need to slow down with his transition to preschool. It's crucial that you let Bobby take his time to integrate into the preschool rather than forcing him to be a "big boy" and expecting him to immediately join in with the other children. During the transition period, try to stay with him at school and slowly increase the time that you are not in direct contact with him. You should also choose a small, less-stimulating preschool where the teachers are understanding of Bobby's sensitivity and where he can develop a secure bond with the teachers. It's better for you to have less income for a few months during a slower transition period than to have Bobby experience anxiety that could possibly have a negative emotional impact on his life.

Question: *Peter, a sensitive high school student, told me during a counseling session: "I seem to always have problems finding a girlfriend. The girls I know always want to be just friends instead of having a romantic relationship. I think most of these girls like the extroverted, aggressive guys, and I'm very shy. I don't like to party that much, so maybe some of the girls think I'm not much fun to be around. However, they seem to always come to me for advice."*

Answer: As you get older you'll find women come to really appreciate your sensitivity. Many sensitive men have told me that their temperament is actually an advantage when meeting women, since it helps them to be mature, responsible, and more expressive than other men. Highly sensitive men understand their partners' needs, and more mature girls and women will appreciate this benefit.

It's important to make your intentions clear to girls when you first meet them. When you meet a girl who interests you romantically, gently but firmly let her know that you would rather be her boyfriend than her confidant. You should also choose to have relationships with girls who are understanding and empathetic toward your sensitivity.

While many high-school girls may think they want a more aggressive boy to date, the more mature and sensitive girls will appreciate all you have to offer. Try to be patient—your time will come.

Question: *My son is in fifth grade and his school counselor told me that he has ADHD— attention-deficit/hyperactivity disorder—and should be on medication. But after learning about the trait of high sensitivity, I'm not sure if he has ADHD or if he's just highly sensitive. He's always been shy and has had an aversion to noise, bright lights, and violence, which are characteristics of the highly sensitive child. His teacher said that he has trouble concentrating in class, yet at home he's able to do his homework without a problem. How can I tell if he has ADHD or is just sensitive?*

Answer: Children with ADHD exhibit inattention, hyperactivity, and impulsivity. Some clinicians may incorrectly diagnose a child with ADHD if he shows any of these characteristics. A sensitive child may, for example, have trouble concentrating as a reaction to classroom over-stimulation. Since ADHD is the most commonly diagnosed psychiatric disorder in children, affecting about three to five percent of children (mostly boys), many sensitive boys may be misdiagnosed (Polanczyk et al., 2007). However, high sensitivity in children is a trait affecting approximately twenty percent of all children (Aron, 1996).

While your son could have ADHD, the vast majority of sensitive children are not ADHD. Most children diagnosed with ADHD are risk-takers, which is at the opposite end of the spectrum from the sensitive boy, who likes to pause and reflect before acting. The ADHD child usually continues to be distracted even in a stimuli-free environment. However, like your son, the sensitive boy may have trouble concentrating in a noisy classroom but is able to focus in a quiet environment at home.

Question: *I've known for a long time that my twelve-year-old son, Ethan, is very sensitive to pain, but now it's gotten so bad that he refuses to go to see the dentist. My husband said we should just force him to go or his dental problems will get worse. He has a cavity that needs to be filled, but he gets extremely upset when I tell him that he has to go to the dentist. Although he hates getting shots at the doctor's office, he doesn't seem to mind it as much as going to the dentist. One problem may be that our dentist told Ethan that his behavior makes it harder for the dentist to work on his teeth. However, I've noticed that his pediatrician has a gentle bedside manner.*

Answer: Some of your son's fears about going to the dentist may be related to the way your dentist has interacted with him. Pedodontists are dentists who specialize in working with children and are trained to deal with kids who are afraid of dental work. I suggest that you speak to some other dentists about your son's sensitivity and fears, and find one who is receptive to your son's sensitivity.

You may want to take him to meet the new, empathetic dentist before his first appointment so he can become familiar with the dentist and the office. You could consider giving your son some herbal or allopathic medicine to lessen his anxiety prior to the appointment, with the dentist's approval. Let the dentist know some of your son's interests so that he could discuss those topics with him during treatment, which will lessen his anxiety. It may increase your son's trepidation of going to the dentist if he gets nervous when a dentist makes him look inside his mouth with a mirror. Since you mentioned that your son can tolerate receiving injections, having the dentist administer an analgesic like Novocain to reduce his pain would also be helpful to reduce his stress during dental treatment. Finally, it could also help if your son listens to his favorite relaxing music with his headset during the appointment.

Question: *I'm a junior in high school, and getting good grades is really important to me because I want to get into a first-rate college. My mom* *recently told me that she thinks that I have the trait of high sensitivity. I have a hard time answering questions while other people are watching me, and I like to take my time in completing tests and written assignments in class. My English teacher constantly criticizes me for working too slowly, and when I've given a wrong answer he makes sarcastic remarks. I get nervous now just entering English class, and I'm afraid to answer any questions in front of the class. I'm worried that if I tell my guidance counselor or the principal, my teacher will give me a bad grade.*

Answer: Your English teacher sounds like an insensitive bully. You and your parents should meet with the principal and your school counselor to discuss this untenable situation. You should come to the meeting prepared with detailed statements and dates about your teacher's behavior. It would also be helpful to have at least one other student corroborate your stories.

You and your parents could also tell the principal and guidance counselor that you have the trait of high sensitivity and show them the list of tips for teachers from Elaine Aron's book, *The Highly Sensitive Person* (1996). Since twenty percent of the population is highly sensitive, there are probably other students who are having similar problems with your teacher. The bottom line is that you should not tolerate emotional abuse from any teacher. If the teacher does not change his behavior, you should transfer to a different class.

Question: *Since I started college last fall, I've been having a terrible time falling asleep. I've always had some sleep problems, but now it's so bad that I'm sleep-deprived. I'm living in a noisy college dorm, yet my roommate and other friends seem to easily fall asleep while I'm wide awake at night. I wake up when I hear noises in the hallway, and even the door to the bathroom banging shut can wake me up. I am desperate for a good night's sleep. It's kind of embarrassing, because nothing seems to bother the other guys and I feel like a wimp if I ask people to keep the noise down in the dorm.*

Answer: In my book *The Highly Sensitive Person's Survival Guide* (2004), there is a chapter with excellent tips for reducing insomnia. I also have further information about healing insomnia on my website, www.drtedzeff.com. Unfortunately, living in a college dorm rarely meets the criteria to create restful sleep by having a quiet, dark, peaceful bedroom. You will need to implement a special sleep program while living in your dorm. Try to develop an evening routine that incorporates some of the following:

- Try to go to bed early.

- Meditate or do progressive relaxation.

- Read an uplifting book.

- Do not look at a clock after 9 P.M.

- Wear an eye mask.

- Tune out noise by using a white-noise sound machine or fan, or try wearing ear plugs or earmuff-style noise-reduction headsets that construction workers use.

Alas, if after trying some of these tips for healing insomnia you're still having problems, you might want to seriously consider an alternative living arrangement.

Question: *I just got home from another meeting with my son's fifth-grade teacher, and I'm furious. I've been trying to explain to her for the last two months that my son is highly sensitive. I even showed her the "tips for teachers" section in Elaine Aron's book,* The Highly Sensitive Child. *However, this teacher is so rigid that she refuses to make any allowances for my son's sensitivity, and he is having a terrible time in school this year. Every day he complains that he hates his teacher and doesn't want to go to school. The principal refuses to transfer him to one of the other fifth-grade* *classes, saying they are already too crowded. I know you believe that even one humiliating experience by a teacher could damage a sensitive boy's educational career and lower his self-esteem. I don't want to see my son put up with his inflexible teacher anymore, but I don't know what to do. We can't afford to pay for a private school.*

Answer: Highly sensitive children frequently feel overwhelmed in school with its attendant stimulation and pressure to perform well. Since many HSBs don't fit in with the eighty percent non-sensitive children, they may feel anxious, alienated, and alone in school. It's challenging enough for an HSB to try to learn in a large public-school classroom, but the situation can becomes virtually unbearable if the teacher refuses to be understanding and work with the sensitive boy's trait.

Since your son's teacher is not receptive to respecting your son's sensitivity and the principal won't change his class, you need to look into alternative academic environments for your son. Is it possible for your son to attend another school near your house? There are many alternative schools and local progressive private schools that would likely be more conducive to your son's emotional and educational needs than his current classroom. Many private schools have scholarships or special programs where parents could pay a lower tuition for working at the school. You could also look into the possibility that your local school district, county, or state could help pay for some of the tuition, since your son's needs are not being met at his local public school. If you're unable to find an affordable private school that meets your son's needs, you may want to seriously consider homeschooling your son.

Question: *My eight-year-old son spends most of his time in his room playing with his electronic games, using his computer, or watching TV. I think this behavior actually makes him more anxious and depressed than he would be otherwise. He is a sensitive boy and something of a homebody who generally avoids going outside. However, he recently returned home from his first backpacking trip with his friend and his friend's family. He looked like a different person when he returned, smiling and full of energy* *and enthusiasm. My husband and I are not the backpacking type, and I don't want to impose on my son's friend's family to take him again. However, I would really like to see him look as happy and energetic as he did when he returned from that backpacking trip.*

Answer: The quiet, beauty, and peace in nature are the perfect antidote for the boy who has been glued to stimulating electronic devices. Even if you and your husband don't like backpacking, you could always go for a walk in nature with your son or visit your local parks. If you don't like going for hikes, you can help your son enjoy nature around your house by planting a garden or reading a book together about the wonders of nature.

Your son could also flourish spending time in nature in a Scout group, provided that the leader is sensitive to your son's needs and the other children treat him kindly. There are also probably local nature-oriented programs that your son could participate in. If you don't want to impose on your son's friend's family, you could always reciprocate for their taking your son backpacking by having your son's friend spend the night at your house.

Chapter 11

Direct to You: Advice from Thirty Sensitive Men

This final chapter is a compilation of the responses of thirty sensitive men from five different countries to the question: "What could your parents, teachers, and other adults have done differently that would have helped you to have had a more positive childhood?" Please make sure to note any of the suggestions that could benefit the HSB in your life.

Accept Your Sensitive Boy Exactly as He Is

Many of the men in my study wanted the adults in their life to have had acknowledged their sensitivity as a positive trait when they were young. Jonathan emphasized, "If you have a sensitive boy, don't look at him as if there's something wrong with him that has to be changed. Instead, adults should view his sensitivity as a special quality, which he can utilize to achieve many positive goals in life. I would tell parents, teachers, and family members of sensitive males that the sensitive boy in their life is a gift from God. They should cherish their sensitive boy and realize that boys like him will become the men that will help heal the planet. They should encourage their sensitive boy to speak his truth and not feel ashamed of who he is. Love your sensitive boy as unconditionally as possible, and encourage him to engage in activities that he's drawn to."

Steve echoed Jonathan's sentiments that adults need to accept the sensitive boy exactly as he is. "I would tell parents and teachers that they should never shame a boy for expressing his emotions. They need to accept the truth that even though their sensitive boy may be different from other guys, there is absolutely nothing wrong with him. He is perfect exactly as he is. Never compare your sensitive son to non-sensitive boys or you will demoralize him. Look for your boy's many positive attributes. Don't push a highly sensitive boy to do something that you know is uncomfortable for him. If I had one thing to tell parents, teachers, family, and friends of a sensitive male, it's that they shouldn't expect him to act like you if you're not highly sensitive."

Don't Force Your HSB to Play Team Sports

I've heard about many a father who tried to force his son to compete in team sports, which is not suited to the temperament of many sensitive boys. Jorgen from Denmark told me, "My dad tried to make me join my school's soccer team, which caused many arguments and hurt our relationship. My dad was a soccer star when he was in school, and even now much of his free time is spent going to soccer matches or watching soccer on television. I felt bad about myself for not wanting to join the soccer team, like I wasn't a real boy. I needed the space to be myself instead of being rejected for not going along with what my dad thought I should do. A father needs to back off from pushing his son to play sports if he doesn't want to."

Don't Act Like Your HSB Has a Pathology or Disorder

While it's important for parents of an HSB to acknowledge their son's trait, the adults in an HSB's life shouldn't label him as if he has a diagnosed emotional disorder. Jonathan said, "I am very leery of making a personality trait or characteristic into a disorder. When I first read some of the books about highly sensitive people, I felt like they were a sort of invitation to avoid greatness. In other words, claiming your trait as a disability or excuse not to try your best won't be helpful in the end. Avoid labeling your HSB or even thinking of him as off or abnormal, as this could potentially make him into a victim and diminish his desire to grow. Putting his sensitivity into the correct context will help him see the great benefits this trait offers and will help give him the courage to excel.

Let Your HSB Know that He's Strong

I remember once seeing a T-shirt that read, "Gentleness is strength." Teach your sensitive son that aggressive and combative behavior is not real strength. Real strength is acting like a fully functional human being, exemplified by being able to express one's full range of emotions. Terry concurred: "I would like parents to know that each sensitive boy is powerful, even though this strength may appear in different ways than in most boys. The parents of an HSB should teach their son that when he shows compassion and gentleness toward people he is demonstrating a different kind of strength. Who's to say that a boy who is caring and gentle is weaker than a boy who likes to fight? As a matter of fact, look at the compassion and tenderness of Christ. He said to turn the other cheek rather than fight back, and his nonviolent message has endured for thousands of years. If an HSB's parents could convey to their son how much inner power he has, that boy would become more confident."

Teach Your Son to Set Boundaries

In the chapter on boys and sports I described how Tyler, a fearful and emotionally sensitive boy, took aikido lessons. This discipline helped him become a more confident boy who could set boundaries. It's vital that adults teach the HSBs in their lives how to set boundaries and how to stand up to aggressive, combative children. Sensitive boys need to learn that they should never tolerate anyone emotionally or physically abusing them.

Tom recalled, "I wish my dad or someone else had taught me how to stand up for myself when I was a frightened, skinny boy in elementary and middle school. However, there was no one available to show me what to do. It really would have helped if I'd learned karate or lifted weights, which would have given me more confidence and made be feel powerful. Parents really need to teach the timid, sensitive boy how to stand up to aggressive bullies, or he'll get picked on in school. I think it's crucial for sensitive boys to toughen up, even though it may be against their nature."

Discipline Gently

As I pointed out earlier in the book, sensitive boys do better with gentle discipline. Harsh discipline can crush the spirit and self-esteem of a sensitive boy. Aaron's parents were strict disciplinarians and punished all of their sons in the same stern manner. Aaron said, "My parents shouldn't have been so harsh and rigid when they disciplined me. My brothers used to laugh off the scolding, but I was deeply hurt by their severe reprimands. Since I craved their acceptance, all my parents had to do was gently tell me that what I had done was wrong, and I probably would have changed. With a sensitive boy, a little discipline goes a long way. It devastated me when my dad used to criticize me in front of others. I still remember an incident when my dad and I were in a crowded store and I accidentally broke a toy. He started screaming at me in front of everyone, shouting about what a clumsy idiot I was. It hurts me to this day to think of that awful experience. Parents should discipline their sensitive children in a gentle, constructive manner—and in private."

Interacting with your sensitive boy in a fair and constructive way means putting his concerns and needs first, rather than reacting according to your own feelings of shame, embarrassment, or frustration. Aaron's dad may have felt embarrassed or aggravated by his son's mistake, making him overreact and damage Aaron. Instead, take a step back, acknowledge your own feelings as a parent, and try to see that these emotions are yours, not a result of your son's shortcomings. Then you will be freer to discipline your HSB in a calm, gentle, and constructive way.

Limit Media Exposure

Ninety percent of the HSMs in my study reported that they did not like watching violence on TV and in the movies when they were young. Since sensitive boys absorb stimuli so deeply, it's important to limit the amount of time that your son is exposed to violent or overstimulating TV shows, movies, and video games.

Parents of a five-year-old HSB told me that when they eliminated television and movies, their son became less moody and more cheerful. Reducing or eliminating visual media in your home will mean that you will need to be more attentive to your child, which can sometimes seem difficult or too time-consuming. However, less time with the electronic babysitter also means more opportunities for fun, joy, and understanding as a family. It may feel like a hard transition at first, but the rewards for the family will be priceless.

Steve recalled, "As a boy, I had a TV in my room that I would watch constantly, since I didn't go out much. I think that watching TV negatively affected my nervous system and probably contributed to my anxiety. I remember that when we used to visit my grandparents house in the summer, where we weren't allowed to watch television, I always felt more peaceful.

"I also think that watching all the images of tough, macho men had a negative impact on me, making me feel worse about myself. Because I felt like I couldn't measure up to those tough guys and they were all I was seeing on TV, I started to feel like there was something wrong with me. Till this day whenever I watch a violent or emotionally upsetting movie, I wake up with bad dreams. I just can't forget about the show after watching it and sometimes the intensity stays with me for days. Although I would have balked at the time, I now wish my parents would have restricted my television viewing."

Help Your HSB Balance Alone Time with Socializing

Sensitive boys need to know that they have a safe, quiet space at home where they can retreat when they're feeling overstimulated, yet they should be gently encouraged to go out in the world if they spend almost all their time alone. Brian noted, "While it's vital that the sensitive boy has downtime, I think he also needs to balance his need for privacy with positive interactions with others. I spent too much time alone when I was a boy. It probably would have been better if my parents encouraged me to go out more. I probably would have been slightly uncomfortable at first, but it would have been good for me in the long run to have spent more time with friends. So maybe the key is that a parent should encourage his or her son to go out more without forcing him. I guess it's a delicate balance."

Not only can a parent gently encourage his or her HSB to venture out into the world a bit more, but the mom or dad can work to facilitate this. When he's younger, you can set up play dates with other children (as long as they treat your HSB respectfully). You can even have the dates at your house if your son feels more comfortable having you around while he plays. You can also sign him up for classes that he'll enjoy: art, music, soccer, or self-defense which will get him out of the house and interacting with other kids and adults. When your boy is a little older, you can support his social life by taking him out for pizza or a movie with small groups of his friends. You may have to work to fade into the background a bit, but making it easy for your son to socialize will help give him the confidence he needs to go out solo next time.

Take a Hike

The sensitive men in my study reported that they really enjoyed spending time in nature, and many HSMs told me that their main refuge from overstimulation and stress as a boy was spending time in a natural setting. Terry fondly remembered, "Hanging out in the woods near my home was the only way I found peace and security from all the chaos at school and at home. Thank God I lived near a forest preserve."

Gary nostalgically expressed the benefits of his walks in nature with his grandfather. "It seems like my parents were always too busy for me, but some of my fondest memories from childhood involved exploring the countryside next to my grandpa's house. We would spend many happy hours observing nature during our hikes. This may sound strange to say, but at the end of our walks my heart would be overflowing with love. I think every sensitive boy would benefit from spending time in nature, especially with a caring adult."

Look Inside Yourself

Perhaps one of the best ways a grown-up can help the HSB in his or her life is to examine how they developed their belief system about how a boy should behave. As Terry so eloquently stated, "If my parents had looked at themselves and dealt with their own dragons, it would have helped me. I think that the best thing parents can do to help their children is to work on their emotional issues instead of projecting their emotional baggage onto their kids. Trying to force your HSB to conform to your value system is more about your feelings than what's right for your boy.

"Parents as well as teachers should realize that everyone is different and what may appear abnormal for male behavior is, in fact, totally normal for a sensitive boy. Adults need to spend some time thinking about how they developed their beliefs about masculinity and whether those beliefs really serve them, their kids, or the world. I mean, is it really so important that men be aggressive, tough, and unemotional? I believe that when parents give these beliefs some serious thought, they'll be more inclined to honor their sons exactly as they are."

Educate Others About Your Son's Trait

As the parent of a sensitive boy, go ahead and inform family, friends, neighbors, and educators that, although your son has the trait of high sensitivity, he is perfectly normal. Jonathan sent me the following e-mail: "When I found your first book, *The Highly Sensitive Person's Survival Guide*, and Dr. Aron's *The Highly Sensitive Person*, I was truly relieved that there are other people in the world who share my trait of sensitivity. Previously, I always thought that I was the only one who was so sensitive, which made me feel pretty messed up. I think it's the duty of adults to let others know that twenty percent of all boys have a finely tuned nervous system."

The more awareness you can spread about this trait, the more you will have helped your son and society. If someone tells you that your son is too sensitive, you could calmly respond, "According to research by Dr. Elaine Aron, highly sensitive people comprise approximately twenty percent of the population (equally divided between male and female). This population has a more finely tuned central nervous system, so they are more susceptible to environmental stimuli, both positive or negative. The stimuli could be noise, fragrance, certain foods, chaos, beauty, or pain. Sensitive boys tend to process sensory stimuli more deeply than other boys. It can be both an enjoyable and challenging trait to have."

One note of caution is that it's important to use your discrimination when sharing information about your son's trait. If you think the other person would ridicule or discount his sensitivity, it's best not to discuss it with them. You could simply respond to someone's caustic remarks about your son's behavior by unequivocally stating that you really enjoy your son's sensitivity, compassion, and kindness.

Conclusion

While *The Strong, Sensitive Boy* is now coming to an end, your work in helping your son to become a strong, confident, happy man is just beginning. I'm sure that as you begin to use the suggestions in this book, you will start to see a positive change in your son. Remember that you're not alone. There are millions of parents of sensitive boys out there trying to help their sensitive sons cope in a world that does not appreciate sensitivity in males.

The time has come to break the outdated, rigid boy code that insists that all boys should be aggressive, thick-skinned, and unemotional. Once you implement the suggestions in this book, your son will be better able to appreciate his sensitivity and successfully navigate through the aggressive boy culture. As your sensitive boy feels stronger and more self-assured, he will be empowered to help make this world a better place for everyone. Working together, you and your son can become integral to making a more peaceful, healthy planet where all males will eventually become fully functioning human beings—exhibiting sensitivity, compassion, and vulnerability.

My best wishes for you and the sensitive boy in your life. May you both have a life filled with joy, good health, and inner-strength.

Appendix: Research Results

This chapter details the results of my research about highly sensitive boys based on in-depth interviews with thirty highly sensitive men from five countries. Though I've cited these results throughout the book, I wanted to offer you the hard data all in one place. This appendix may help clarify some of the results and will enable you to look back on the information with ease.

Although my study included a small sample of thirty highly sensitive men, and a larger sample of sensitive men needs to be completed to obtain statistically significant data, the initial results indicates the following interesting trends:

- The highly sensitive males from North America (U.S. and Canada) who reported that they had supportive parents as boys (indicated by at least one parent always being supportive of their sensitivity) and who played group sports as boys were "never" or "rarely" teased for being sensitive.

- The North American sensitive males who regularly participated in team sports, regardless of their physique, were "never" or "rarely" teased.

- However, the North American HSMs who reported that neither parent was supportive of their sensitivity and who never played team sports as boys were "usually" or "always" teased by other children.

- The research indicated that eighty-five percent of sensitive boys did not participate in team sports and reported that throughout their lives, they preferred to participate in individual exercise.

- Eighty-five percent of HSMs "always" avoided fighting when they were boys, with the remaining fifteen percent responding that they "usually" avoided fighting. As they were growing up, ninety percent of the HSMs did not like watching violence on television or in movies.

- There are important cultural variations for HSBs growing up in different countries. The HSMs from India, Thailand, and most of those from Denmark stated that they were "never" or "rarely" teased as boys for their sensitivity, regardless of the variables of supportive parents or participation in team sports.

- The HSMs from Thailand and India indicated that they "usually" or "always" had many friends growing up, while virtually all of the HSMs who grew up in North America indicated that they had few if any friends. The exceptions were the North American HSBs who participated in team sports.

- Regardless of the country where the HSB grew up, seventy-five percent indicated that, as boys, they usually or always thought that there was something wrong with them. Even some of the HSMs who reported that their parents supported their sensitivity and that they had positive peer interactions felt there was something wrong with them.

- Ninety percent of the HSMs felt that they hadn't fit in with other boys.

- Ninety-five percent of the HSMs in my study indicated that they "usually" or "always" have been: intuitive, gentle, responsible, a peacemaker, and good at counseling people.

- My research indicated that ninety-five percent of the HSMs in my survey are heterosexual.

References

Aron, Elaine. 1996. *The Highly Sensitive Person*. New York: Carol Publishing.

———. 1999. *The Highly Sensitive Person's Workbook*. New York: Broadway Books.

———. 2001. *The Highly Sensitive Person in Love*. New York: Broadway Books.

———. 2002. *The Highly Sensitive Child*. New York: Broadway Books.

Baron-Cohen, Simon. 2004. *The Essential Difference: Male and Female Brains and the Truth About Autism*. New York: Basic Books.

Bhat, Naras. 1995. *How To Reverse and Prevent Heart Disease and Cancer*. Burlingame, CA: Kumar Pati.

Bowlby, J. 1973. *Attachment and Loss*. New York: Basic Books.

Canfield, Jack, Mark Victor Hansen, Kimberly Kirberger, and Mitch Claspy. 1997. *Chicken Soup for the Teenage Soul: 101 Stories of Life, Love, and Learning*. New York: HCI Teens.

Carpenter, Deborah. 2009. *The Everything Parents Guide to Dealing with Bullies.* Avon, MA: Adams Media.

Chen,, Xinyin, Kenneth Rubin, Yuerong Sun.1992. Social reputation and peer relationships in Chinese and Canadian children. *Child Development* 63:1336-43.

Crawford, Catherine. 2009. *The Highly Intuitive Child.* Alameda, CA: Hunter House.

Dobbs, David. 2009. The Science of Success. *The Atlantic Magazine,* December.

Dyer, Wayne. 2009. *The Power of Intention.* PBS Television Series.

Gurian, Michael. 1996. *The Wonder of Boys.* New York: Tarcher.

———. 2007. *The Minds of Boys.* San Francisco: Jossey-Bass.

Harkness, Sarah, C.Super, M.Bloor, B. Muller, and B. Moscardino. September, 2000. The cultural meanings of temperamet dimensions: findings from the international study of parents, children and schools. Paper presented at the occasional temperament conference. Westbrook, Connecticut.

Kindlon, Dan and Michael Thompson. 2000. *Raising Cain.* New York: Ballantine.

Kinsey, Alfred. 1998. *Sexual Behavior in the Human Male.* Bloomington, IN: Indiana University Press.

Kivel, Paul. 1992. *Men's Work.* Center City, MN: Hayelden.

Kupers, Terry. 1993. *Revisioning Men's Lives.* New York: Guilford Press.

Kurtz, R. 1990. *Body-Centered Psychotherapy: The Hakomi Method.* Mendocino, CA: LifeRhythm.

Lad, Vasant. 1984. *Ayurveda: The Science of Self-Healing.* Wilmot, WI: Lotus Light.

Levine, Peter. 1997. *Waking The Tiger: Healing Trauma.* Berkeley, CA: North Atlantic Books.

Paramatmananda, Swami, 2001. *Talks by Swami Parmatmananda.* San Ramon, CA: M.A. Center.

Pelletier, Kenneth. 1977. *Mind as Healer, Mind as Slayer.* New York: Delacorte.

Pittman, Frank. 1994. *Man Enough.* New York: Perigee Trade.

Polanczyk G., M.S. de Lima, B.L. Horta, J. Biederman, L.A. Rohde. 2007. The worldwide prevalence of ADHD: A systematic review and metaregression analysis. *The American Journal of Psychiatry* 164 (6): 9428.

Pollack, William. 1998. *Real Boys.* New York: Random House.

Pope, Harrison, Katherine Phillips, and Roberto Olivardia. 2002. *The Adonis Complex.* Tampa, FL: Free Press.

Ryan, Caitlan, David Hubner, Rafael Diaz, Jorge Sanchez. 2009. Family rejection as a predictor of negative health outcomes in white and latino lesbian, gay, and bisexual young adults. *Journal of the American Academy of Pediatrics* 123 (1): 346-352.

Thomas, Marlo. 1972. *Free To Be You and Me.* New York: Arista Records.

Tolle, Eckhart. 1999. *The Power of Now*. Novato, CA: New World Library.

Tonja R. Nansel, Mary Overpeck, Ramani S. Pilla, W. June Ruan, Bruce Simons-Morton, Peter Scheidt. 2001. Bullying behaviors among U.S. youth: Prevalence and association with psychosocial adjustment. *Journal of the American Medical Association* 285:2094-2100.

Zeff, Ted. 1981. *The Psychological and Physiological Effects of Meditation and the Physical Isolation Tank on the Type A Behavior Pattern*. Ann Arbor,
MI: University Microfilms.

———. 2004. *The Highly Sensitive Person's Survival Guide*. Oakland, CA: New Harbinger Publications.

About the Author

Ted Zeff, Ph.D., received his doctorate in psychology in 1981 from the California Institute of Integral Studies in San Francisco, CA. He is the author of *The Highly Sensitive Person's Survival Guide* and *The Highly Sensitive Person's Companion*. He currently teaches workshops and consults internationally on coping strategies for highly sensitive people and sensitive boys. For more information please visit his web site, www.drtedzeff.com